Moving to Small Town America

How To Find & Fund the Home of Your Dreams

WILLIAM SEAVEY

Real Estate
Education Company
a division of Dearborn Financial Publishing, Inc.

This publication is designed to provide accurate and authoritative information in regard to the subject matter covered. It is sold with the understanding that the publisher is not engaged in rendering legal, accounting or other professional service. If legal advice or other expert assistance is required, the services of a competent professional person should be sought.

Acquisitions Editor: Christine Litavsky
Managing Editor: Jack Kiburz
Interior Design: Lucy Jenkins
Cover Design: Rohani Design

Printed in the United States of America

96 97 98 10 9 8 7 6 5 4 3 2 1

Library of Congress Cataloging-in-Publication Data

Seavey, William.
    Moving to small town America : how to find and fund the home of your dreams / William Seavey.
        p.   cm.
    Includes index.
    ISBN 0-7931-1427-6 (pbk.)
        1. Cities and towns—United States.   2. Relocation (Housing)—United States.   3. Quality of life—United States.   4. Country life—United States.
    I. Title.
HT123.S387   1996
307.76'0973—dc20   95-37742

Contents

Preface

What you are reading has been at least four years from conception to execution. The actual writing took only about three months. The rest of the time was spent trying to get the concept marketed!

Most of the "escape-the-city books" published in recent years have been self-published because the authors hit a brick wall with mainstream publishing houses. Believe me, I know most of the authors and some of the tales they tell.

The news media, on the other hand, have quite passionately embraced our efforts to help urban "opt outs." We would probably have been out of business long ago without their help. A few courageous writers, reporters and editors made much out of our rural relocation firm, the Greener Pastures Institute, long before we, ourselves, could predict that we would fulfill the orders we got without going bankrupt. Now our work has been publicized in such respected places as *The Wall Street Journal, Good Housekeeping* magazine, *The New York Times* and the *L.A. Times*. But all the publicity never resulted in a book offer.

Obviously, I am grateful to Dearborn Publishing and my editor Chris Litavsky in particular for believing in this book. They picked it out of a stack of unsolicited outlines. They also published the excellent book, *Finding and Buying Your Place in the Country* (originally published in the late 1970s) by Les Scher, so I am proud to be associated with Dearborn.

Years ago I determined (at least for myself) that living in our biggest cities was, for many, not conducive to overall personal well being. In the course of gathering data on the drawbacks of cities, I have naturally developed a fairly sophisticated understanding of the reasons why. Yet many people instinctively know the reasons—population density, threats to personal safety, pollution, lack of family orientation, disconnectedness from land and resources, unneighborliness, etc. Greener Pastures Institute (GPI) has reached perhaps 250,000 people through its publications, classes, counseling and consulting since its birth as Relocation Research in Bend, Oregon (which the *Oregonian* newspaper recently called Oregon's boomingest town). And we talk to people daily about their frustrations with urban areas, particularly those over 500,000 population.

We network with nearly everyone who is trying to educate people about big city negatives and small city/town positives. A few, like us, feel a strong compulsion to make people aware of why, for many people, most large urban areas simply don't work today. I don't think we've ever made a dime (at least directly) reminding people that big cities are a relatively new phenomenon, and that there are things we can do today to make them more sustainable—or, for those who want to start over in a different place, to *keep* communities sustainable. (The new "communitarian" movement holds some promise, and we are beginning to write about that.) Most of those who come to us are desperate souls whom we have to rein in and tell to, "slow down, you need to think about all the options, and do some long-term planning."

A few in our network are trying to get rich quickly by selling urban opt-out materials, but most are sincere in their various approaches, which range from publishing newsletters on how to "downscale" your life to encouraging corporations to set up more telecommuting programs. But, if any of it helps people live in environments in which they can breathe clean air, get off the nine-to-five treadmill and have a family life again, we get behind it in some way. The truth is, that big city excesses are to a large extent at the root of our national disenfranchisement—which extends from politics to child raising.

Too many of us, like myself in the early 1970s, feel compelled to work (and therefore to live) in the big metros. By the time we are in our 30s, extricating ourselves proves challenging indeed. Fortunately, I abandoned large urban areas (except for a few short stretches) early on, though there have nevertheless been plenty of ups and downs in my personal fortunes. Please don't accuse me of failing in the big cities; I was an advertising copywriter with *McCall's* magazine at the tender age of 23 and worked in New York City as a Magazine Publisher's Association intern at 21. But you don't have to demonstrate your competence or competitiveness anymore by "going metro." Plenty of smaller cities and towns are excellent proving grounds, as we shall see.

It is downright scary what's in store for us in the next few decades. The World Future Society predicts that by the year 2100, 90 percent of the world's population will live in urban areas compared with 52 percent now (77 percent in the United States). Do we really think that man is meant—or at least destined—to reside where there is more concrete than dirt, more fellow competitive *Homo sapiens* than members of the animal and plant kingdoms, foul air and clogged freeways, and random violence caused essentially by lack of time or freedom to teach values? Perhaps the World Future Society's projections are based on the premise that we will continue down the path of industrialization and modernism, which requires lots of bodies to run machines, traditionally in urban centers. But with population growing so fast over the globe, where will there be room for these bodies?

I hope that Greener Pastures is part of an alternative vision that will eventually see us limiting our population to no more than two children per family, and that a general recognition will arise that the best place to raise a family, work for ourselves or others and develop a satisfying lifestyle is in "the country," places fairly distant from the megalopolises many of us reside in today. Decentralization/dispersal makes a lot of sense to me, and increasingly to others—especially now that sophisticated telecommunications and independent energy sources (like solar power) allow us to run enterprises just about anywhere we please. This is a true revolution in how we live our lives and see our world (about time!), and one we are proud to be associated with.

Moving to Small Town America won't bore you, however, with a lot of philosophizing and proselytizing about *why* you should give up being a city slicker. Many of you have a pretty innate sense of that already. But a lot of you have confided to me in interviews that wanting to "go rural" is a dirty little secret heretofore revealed to only a few (and certainly not to a professional). It shouldn't have to be.

I appreciate the fact that many of you who are attracted to this book, however, are at various stages of readiness to make a move. Some of you will conclude that it isn't possible or desirable, at least not anytime soon. And it is not easy to pull up stakes when what some people call common sense dictates that you should stay put. The early chapters will examine the pros and cons, and succeeding chapters—for those serious about getting on track—will offer hard data and inspiration to get you packing. If that seems prudent.

Sincerely,

William L. Seavey
April 1995

"If cities did not exist, it would be necessary to invent them."
—John Naisbitt, *Megatrends 2000*

Acknowledgments

*M*oving *to Small Town America* has been a collaborative effort with help from many quarters. Many thanks go to my parents, William H. Seavey and Annette B. Seavey, who have had abiding faith in their son's efforts, even if they have not always agreed with his methods.

To my wife, Laurel, who has had many good suggestions for the book and the patience to tolerate my many hours in front of a computer (which neither of us likes!).

To my son, Erik, who has always appreciated the work Daddy does, even during the lonely year we have been forced to be apart.

To Chris Litavsky, my editor, who has always been courteous and considerate, full of bright ideas, and willing to give me a little slack around deadline time.

And to all of you who have inspired and energized the content of *Moving to Small Town America*: Len and Beverly de Geus, John Shuttleworth, J. D. Belanger, John Schaeffer, Julie Hayward and Ken Spooner, Jack Lessinger, Ph.D., Brad Edmondson, Meg Letterman, Bill Kaysing, Harry Dictor, Paul and Sarah Edwards, David A. Heenan, Irv Thomas, Sheryl Ullman, Margaret Bard, Ph.D., Chuck and Rodica Woodbury, Jack Smith and others too numerous to mention.

Chapter 1

Deciding To Move
to Small Town America

Should you move? As a relocation specialist, I've predicated an entire business—one I basically invented—on the idea that it is often in your best interest to pull up stakes and haul body, soul and personal possessions hundreds if not thousands of miles across the good ol' USA to your "personal Eden."

Yet after doing this for more than ten years I've occasionally had nagging doubts. *U.S. Catholic* magazine once asked for feedback from readers who had moved away from their birthplaces—and sometimes moved back. There were points of view from all sides. Many said they needed to distance themselves from relatives and friends and were quite happy in their new surroundings. Others found the process wrenching and later decided to return "home." Overall, the magazine concluded that moving/relocation wasn't all it was cracked up to be and advised most readers to stay put.

Some years ago a study was conducted that ranked the major life stresses. Death of a spouse or family member and loss of a job, I remember, ranked in the top ten. I also remember that moving was somewhere in the top 20 but noted that a death or job loss might often precipitate a move.

So in reality moving could be seen as stressful on a number of levels and something we should consider very carefully beforehand. Alas, many moves are made hastily, and this exacerbates the stress.

Yet moving is in Americans' blood. (One in five of us changes residences every year, although few moves, comparatively, are interstate.) The entire country was founded on westward expansionism, waves of settlers pushing on as new territories opened up. (It was only about 1900 that the government declared the western frontier to be "gone." We had reached the shores of California and cemented our borders by then.) Interestingly, *The New York Times* declared in 1993 that we have started to reverse course in the 1990s as ex-aerospace workers from the Golden State, and others, have started to migrate eastward into Colorado, Idaho, Nevada, Arizona, Utah, Montana and some of the midwestern states.

REASONS FOR MOVING

Traditionally, we have moved for job advancement reasons. But this is becoming less of an issue today. For one thing, corporations are downsizing and many of us may never work at a traditionally high- or even "good"-paying job again. Writes Peter Francese, publisher of *American Demographics*, "Massive corporate layoffs have changed the focus from employment to personal enterprise. The explosion of entrepreneurs and independent contractors has already begun, and it will gather force as the decade continues."

The extent to which individuals, especially those over age 50, are being pared from corporate roles is confirmed by 10,000 respondents to an American Association of Retired Persons (AARP) survey in late 1994. More than two-thirds indicated they left their jobs under duress, either involuntarily or voluntarily, but under pressure. In one instance 80 employees were laid off, three-fourths of whom were 45 or older.

So if we do move it may not be for advancement but to find a better environment in which to start, franchise or buy an existing business, or simply consummate an early retirement. And whatever we do, we can expect to cope with all sorts of other changes that country living seems to embrace, such as building your own house or hauling your own garbage to the dump.

I'm all for you if you decide to go into business. The author has always felt uncomfortable working for corporations and has run about five small businesses—from a resume-writing service to an apartment maintenance service company—during the course of corporate employment or completely independent of it. And to some degree corporations are picking up on the trends by trying to adapt their workstyles to their valued employees (telecommuting is one example). Others are relocating to the places the "emerging workforce" is going. They are essentially following the working class who insist on better environments for all sorts of reasons. More about that later.

But what if you have a perfectly good job or business where you are? Sure, it's probably in the big city (77 percent of us live in cities of over 50,000 population according to the Census Bureau—easily 50 percent in the truly big metros like Los Angeles, Chicago and New York City). Then the moving issue becomes more than a little dicey even when you are predisposed to consider it. A recent Gallup poll indicated that 29 percent of you would prefer to live in a smaller city of 10,000 to 100,000 population and 52 percent in a rural area or small town. Presumably, a large percentage of those who revealed this bias *also* have secure jobs or businesses. But there is obviously no mass migration going on, though it could certainly be considered a trend and even a movement.

So what goes? Well, naturally many who dislike cities for one reason or another *and* who have good jobs there will *never* move because (1) it is unthinkable to quit a good job even if the inconveniences and/or threats to health in the city are bitter trade-offs; (2) many of your friends and relatives live in the city and you can't imagine leaving them behind; (3) moving to a tropical island, the mountains or the beach is a fantasy that abates a few weeks after you come back from vacation and (4) the money or resources just aren't there to consummate a move.

But the fact is, more and more people are acting on their dreams for three reasons: (1) the biggest cities are truly deteriorating; (2) corporate restructuring is forcing people to make lifestyle changes and (3) the countryside is still basically unspoiled and many new and exciting opportunities are developing there.

Whether you end up moving or not hopefully will have something to do with this book. We want to be devil's advocates to some degree because many moves to rural enclaves crashed and burned in the 60s and 70s—including my own. It was the need for authoritative advice and information on making a city-to-country transition that led to the concept of a national urban opt-out service from the small town of Bend, Oregon, in 1983. And the Greener Pastures Institute has existed ever since.

Statistics can mislead, but we do know that 600,000 Californians left the state in 1993—mostly for a dozen or so interior western states—and that there is a continuing migration to counties throughout the country that are fairly far removed from urban areas. One researcher has dubbed these counties the "penturbs." In a new report by the Bureau of the Census, rural growth between 1990 and 1994 has been shown to be the largest in 20 years and is approaching the record gains of the 70s. The report shows that people are moving to small towns at three times the pace they were in the 1980s!

On second thought, maybe there *is* a mass migration going on . . .

WILL YOU BE ACCEPTED?
MYTHS AND REALITIES OF BECOMING
THE NEW KID ON THE BLOCK

Most of us who hesitate to move who have no fear of leaving or losing a job or business (such as those nearing retirement or recently laid off by a corporation) are nevertheless worried that wherever they end up may turn out to be unfriendly—that it will take years or at least months to break the ice with neighbors, new employers, etc. This will sound strange to those who feel (justifiably, as we shall see later) that city life couldn't be *more* unfriendly! But we count on many small relationships for support these days, and they exist just about everywhere.

Some 15 years ago, after moving to Bend, Oregon, with my family, I canvassed my new neighborhood in an effort to set up a Sunday potluck to get to know people. The potluck was a mild success. But I remember meeting a woman at her doorstep who hadn't ventured out of her house in over a year because she felt intrinsically unwelcome. And she didn't make it to the potluck, either.

It is easy for inertia to set in or, worse, a mindset that just because you are a newcomer you are somehow unworthy. Which may indeed be the case in some of the "mecca"-type towns that many of our clients have targeted on their Eden lists. But generally newcomers are welcome anywhere if they don't insist on bragging about where they just came from and instead project tolerance and appreciation for their new location.

People who seem reticent to fit in are often recent ex-urbanites who have seen their once-livable metros go to ruin, with gridlock, pollution, violence, high taxes and so on. Thus it is on their agenda to make absolutely sure the new place stays "pristine." This sets them up immediately for disappointment. We are constantly telling clients not to think in terms of escaping one place but of *embracing* a *new* one—which may have some flaws but, if smaller and much more rural, will probably be friendlier and more cooperative than the former one.

Some might well question this presumption, however, despite all I have seen in the smaller cities and towns I have lived in and researched. There is a story of a man sitting on the side of the road who sees a traveler come by. He asks the traveler, "What are the people like in yonder village?" The traveler replies, "They are good people, always willing to help each other." The man says that these people sound just like the people in *his* village. Then another traveler comes by and the man asks *him* what the people are like in *his* village. "Some are very nice but others are not so," he replies. The man by the roadside responds that the people in his village are like that, too. Finally, a third traveler comes by and the man asks *him* what the people are like in *his* village. "The people are mean spirited, petty and a gossiping bunch," he says. The man replies that this pretty much describes the people in *his* village, too.

This story would seem to confirm what we know about human nature in the context of our communities—that there are all different kinds of people cohabiting reasonably well. And this is probably true of most smaller communities. Increasingly, though, it is simply not true of our largest metro areas.

And here's the proof if ever there was such. University of California (Fresno) psychology professor Robert V. Levine, Ph.D., dispatched 36 research students to the same number of cities across the nation in 1993 to make comparisons of the average person on the street's treatment of strangers. The goal was to find out why some cities were "friendlier" than others. Researchers would walk down the sidewalk and "accidentally" drop a pen and see if anyone would pick it up and return it to them. Or they would act injured or crippled and see if anyone (à la the Boy Scout code) would help them across a busy street. The results clearly indicated that the largest, *densest* cities, like New York City and Los Angeles (downtown), had the least cooperative people. Another major factor correlating with friendliness was the amount of air pollution, which confirmed an earlier study that smog (combined with heat) tends to exacerbate crime waves.

Obviously, environment does shape our attitudes and behavior. And big cities appear to alter personalities and behavior in negative ways that are hard to deny.

If you move to a small town, another "attitude needing adjustment" has to do with downscaling your expectations about standard of living, ethnicity, weather, school quality and so on. Even if you've done a lot of research on your new locale there will always be surprises. And seeing these factors through city-colored glasses is a guarantee you will either stand out in the crowd or set yourself up for more disappointment. Getting acclimatized is the subject of the last chapter of this book. What's here is just the short course.

*I*mportant Tip . . .

When considering moving to a new place—or even after just moving there—try to suspend your judgment and prejudices. It's natural to view a town through city-colored glasses, but remember, you're not moving in order to replicate *urban* values.

It is true that many places have been hard hit by growth from urban areas in recent years, and this trend is not going to go away. Some residents may truly resent newcomers, and there won't be anything you can do to change their minds. You may be a wonderful person, yet townspeople attitudes may simply be prejudiced against a "Californicator." Bumpers in several rapidly changing western states sport "City Slicker Go Home" epithets, and I have known instances in which newcomers have been cussed out, had rocks thrown at their cars with out-of-state plates, etc. One couple moved to Coeur d' Alene, Idaho, got jobs, and still were the subject of unfriendly remarks and sneers. (The story was reported in the news media and I later interviewed them myself. They eventually returned to California.) But these remain isolated situations.

In the highly popular towns (like the above example) you may well have an uphill battle gaining a footing—but for a variety of reasons these are not good destinations anyway. More about "meccas" in Chapter 3.

On the positive side, some psychologists say that moving can be broadening, encouraging adaptability and personal growth. I have even heard relocation referred to by one therapist as the "geographic cure."

I think of moving as a last resort, despite everything I have read or experienced. There is nothing glamorous or fun about pulling up stakes unless it is to leave a truly unsatisfying, unsupportive situation behind. In an article from the *Utne Reader*, "Make Your Place Your Career," the author was determined to stay in his small city to the extent that he was willing to change jobs and even careers throughout his life to be able to do so. Community, in his opinion, was paramount, and to leave it behind a sacrilege. Even though I'm a "relocation expert," I rather had to concur, and wrote the author to say so. The new "communitarian movement" embraces the stay-put philosophy, and it is one that deserves attention.

But not all of us can literally make our place our career or afford to spend a lot of time undoing the dastardly deeds of our forefathers and foremothers—or, I dare say, even ourselves.

Overpopulation, I believe, is the main bogeyman. Most think of overpopulation as a "third world" problem. But this country nearly doubled in size in the last 50 years (from 150 to 265 million), and most of those numbers poured into the cities and their suburbs from small towns and farms. Actually, it is *urbanization* that causes so much discord because we were never meant to live in huge megalopolises. The way we live today makes it nearly impossible to grow part of our own food, breathe clean air, or get to know our neighbors well. In 1900 there were only 11 cities of over a million population; today there are 275 globally. The marketers in urban areas have what I would call a captive audience—one of the reasons we have become such a materialistic society, although the root cause is our inability or unwillingness to do the things for ourselves, like housebuilding, food preservation, even child raising, that we used to take for granted. (Now others do them for us and we become slaves to corporate or governmental salaries in order to be able to pay them.)

As cities grow even larger and more complex—which they surely will—our personal lives will most assuredly suffer. High costs of housing and living in general do destroy marriages and families. Commuting to jobs far from home contributes to latchkey child raising and few family activities together. Yet I admire those parents who can somehow raise healthy children (and stay sane themselves) living and working in the big city. It is probably the greatest of challenges today.

And most of Greener Pastures' clients in counseling sessions have been parents who are fed up with the lifestyle and the threats to their own and their children's health and well being, I might add. A study by Zero Population Growth confirms that the midsized or second-tier city (population 75,000–200,000 maximum) out in rural areas is best for children and, by extension presumably, their parents. Interestingly, such cities as Rome and Greece during the so-called Golden Age never exceeded 100,000 people. Another item: The Mayans were the only people who ever abandoned their cities on a large scale (they went back to their jungles and live that way to this day). In addition to being threatened by invaders, they simply outstripped their food and water supplies and had no choice. This could be the United States in the not too distant future. A new study by the Carrying Capacity Network in Washington, D.C., confirms that by the year 2050, Americans will have only *half* of the arable land they need to feed themselves if trends in urbanization, highway development, erosion and pollution persist.

We may simply have to argue at this point that many urban places are not fit for man or beast as things stand. Yet, even if you agree that this is the case, it may not, of course, be possible for you to move right away or anytime soon.

Below is a quiz I developed some years ago for Los Angeles residents. In the spirit of not jumping on the bandwagon to encourage out-migration from what I often consider America's worst metro, I proposed that every quality-of-life issue you might have could be framed in two ways depending on certain factors as in the quiz that follows.

*Q*uiz: Should You Move?

(Check those statements that are true for you. Although it is impossible to make a totally intelligent decision to move based on the ratio between the checks under each heading, this is an indicator of the potential success of your move.)

Reasons To Move

❑ Your marriage and family life will be enhanced by the move. Members will work better together because in a less urban setting there is generally more equality and less division of labor.

❑ Smog or pollution in the city is seriously imperiling your health or the health of a family member.

❑ You want an outdoor-oriented career, don't mind working at less skilled occupations (often plentiful in rural areas), or plan to buy a going business.

❑ Crime in your neighborhood has been getting worse for several years and represents a threat to physical, spiritual and psychological well being.

❑ Overall school quality (test scores, funding, etc.) has been in decline in your community for some time with no real prospects for reversal.

❑ You want to benefit from the considerably lower housing costs in a small town or rural area, either because your equity in a current house will go much further or you have been priced out of the local market altogether.

❑ You want to have a better sense of community than is possible in a multiple-city metropolitan area and wish to become active in your community's betterment affairs.

❑ You are not "attached" to cultural and entertainment activities/ amenities of the big city—you can amuse yourself with simpler pleasures, such as hobbies or travel.

❑ You enjoy the weather extremes and variety of many places outside your relatively balmy location and are prepared to pay considerably more for heating and cooling.

❑ You wish to live a less harried lifestyle and are willing to do for yourself many of the things that others supplied you in the city.

Reasons Not To Move

❑ Your marriage and family life have occasional ups and downs like most people's, but despite the pressures of an urban location you are holding your own.

❑ Smog and pollution are irritants but you feel you can live with them at this time.

❑ You are happy in your job or career, can't imagine working outdoors at manual labor and have no interest in taking on the responsibilities of running your own business—at least at this time.

❑ Crime is everywhere but at least in your neighborhood there are Neighborhood Watch groups, a responsive police department and parents who supervise their kids.

❑ School board members, administrators and teachers may not share all your ideas about educating kids but school district quality remains high.

❑ You want to make a killing in rural real estate just as you might do speculating on houses here in the big city.

❑ You know at least some of your neighbors and are taking an active part in local government by serving on a town council, volunteering for a community group, etc.

❑ You like the city's cultural activities and can't imagine being without them, even though they are sometimes inconvenient to get to.

❑ You like the relatively temperate climate where you are now and don't think you could adjust to snow, high altitudes, excessive rain, etc.

❑ You want to reduce the pace of your life for a period of time (take a vacation or go on a retreat).

This will help you determine if big city life is truly the villain or whether you are taking the easy way out (though not really so easy) by fleeing to the countryside. Obviously, my research has led to a bias that big city life *is* the villain, but many would argue that the *extent* of the "villainy" has a lot to do with your personal circumstances, which it obviously does. There are people who thrive in urban settings, although as we age, fewer and fewer find the excitement and challenges worth it.

BEST PROSPECTS FOR A MOVE SOON

Some of us are obviously better candidates for a move to the countryside than others. Parents with young children seem to top the list, confirmed by the Zero Population Growth study referred to above and by Greener Pastures' own client base. Most of the parents we have seen are in their mid to late 30s or early 40s. They may have had a variety of jobs in their careers and are ready to make a transition to something less stressful. Often I talk with women who want to stay at home with their children instead of being forced to work outside to pay the urban bills. (However, they may also want to work part-time and are often interested in a home-based business). Because a couple potentially doubles the amount of adaptability (two heads are better than one) needed to transition to a more rural lifestyle, it often works out. A caveat, however: Teenagers will resist leaving their friends and familiar surroundings and may even resent the move for the duration of their adolescent years. I personally wouldn't want to move them after age 10 or so.

Obviously, retirees or pre-retirees whose children are out of the nest and whose friends or relatives have died or relocated are excellent prospects for a move to a small town. Retirees usually have the independent incomes that will allow them to live anywhere without working, though many take part-time jobs because they are available. Most are very concerned about leaving a metropolis which has diverse medical facilities, but more and more small towns have clinics and even hospitals.

I once wrote an article for *Resident and Family Physician* magazine on why doctors themselves like to practice in certain small towns; many are willing to trade high incomes and heavy patient loads for a better lifestyle. In Bend, Oregon, site of the survey, I learned that they loved to ski, hike and participate in down-home community activities. In fact, a physician was a regular benefactor and volunteer at our church. You hear about small towns looking for doctors, but I've also met a number of doctors (and counseled a few personally) looking for small towns they can relocate to. With or without doctors, people live three to five years longer in smaller towns and rural areas, according to a study called Life Gain.

Single people may do better in smaller towns, especially if they are seeking a mate. Many complain bitterly about the "meat market" in big cities, criticizing the quality of marital candidates. The inability to find a compatible partner is a corollary to why *parents* give up on the cities. Relationships in general are just not very satisfying. A national electric cooperative and the Roper organization did an extensive study on perceptions of family life quality, in which only 4 percent of those polled said cities were good places to raise a family versus 69 percent in smaller towns and rural areas. Of course, not all single people get married or have children even if they find a partner. Single people who are alone may suffer from isolation in smaller towns and rural areas, as one study shows that women do in general. But many single people have come to the Greener Pastures Institute with the hope of living a fairly self-reliant lifestyle—and certainly the countryside is the setting for that. (Many single women are at a considerable disadvantage trying to meet living expenses in the big city, especially since women still make only two-thirds the wages of men.)

Corporate career types may or may not do well in the countryside. In certain industries like finance, commercial real estate and motion pictures, you virtually have to work in the city. (For two years we had an office in the Los Angeles area, and, ironically, many of those in the film, TV and record industry wanted out the most. Yet only the most creative, like the fellow who set up a syndicated radio show that he could do from anywhere, were able to.) If you're in your 20s you might give serious thought to the field you want to work in from the urban versus country angle; my experience is that once you hit 30 you may have had it with the city. Fortunately, there is a trend among corporations to relocate in smaller towns. In the Los Angeles area, nearly 300 corporations relocated between 1990 and 1993 (many, incidentally, going to Idaho). Other corporations, like Wal-Mart, grow up in the countryside and stay there. A few, like one I worked for in Bend, Oregon, which manufactured winterizing systems for RVs and cabins, went to the big city, got the needed capitalization and came back home. And here's a word to the wise for young people: You'll find country employers less cutthroat than city employers, generally, because they're often forced to be more accountable. (And you are too if you plan on doing a lot of job hopping.)

If you've been in business or want to go into business, you may find some unique opportunities in rural areas. You may make less money, but, as I found out, you can have market niches all to yourself. Imagine having the only business of its kind serving a 100-mile area, as I did. I was truly a big fish in a small pond. In the city there are few stones unturned in business, and if you do start something original, there will be imitators galore before you can say "SBA loan." Speaking of which, there are a number of programs sponsored by the government and by city, county and state agencies that encourage rural businesses. These include outright grants and low-interest loans. More about this in the financial game plans chapter.

Whether you feel ready to move to the country tomorrow, next year or never (but you still bought this book to make sure you don't make a mistake), here's a Country Relocation Readiness quiz. It won't tell you if you can survive financially or if your marriage will thrive in a rural setting, but it will rate your attitudes in general, which are often very different among city slickers and so-called country bumpkins.

Country Relocation Readiness Quiz

Respond to each entry by circling Y for Yes, NS for Not Sure or N for no.

Y NS N   1.   Large shopping centers are important to me.

Y NS N   2.   To get a job in a small town I shouldn't need a resume or suit and tie.

Y NS N   3.   Family activities are more important to me than working hard at a job.

Y NS N   4.   I know the difference between a cistern and a septic tank.

Y NS N   5.   I would enjoy being homebound by storms, a gas shortage, a power outage, etc.

Y NS N   6.   My idea of country living is calling in a repair person to fix the washer, car, etc.

Y NS N   7.   Not being fully accepted in my new location threatens my sense of self-worth.

Y NS N   8. The best source of information on a new area is the chamber of commerce.

Y NS N   9. I enjoy taking care of animals and growing fruits and vegetables.

Y NS N   10. I believe I could find ways to reduce my living expenses by up to 50 percent in a rural setting.

Y NS N   11. Having neighbors who don't share my religion, politics, etc. is not a problem to me.

Y NS N   12. I'd like to take an active interest in my community by serving on the town council.

Y NS N   13. I prefer to have others make decisions for me rather than be a self-starter.

Y NS N   14. I get bored easily.

Y NS N   15. I know the difference between a building code and a zoning law.

Y NS N   16. I would have enough money to live without a job for at least a year.

Y NS N   17. I like to take risks.

Y NS N   18. I bought this book already and am not just skimming it at the bookstore or library.

Y NS N   19. I have traveled to or possibly lived in the area of the country to which I'd like to relocate.

Y NS N   20. If my neighbor's dog trespasses on my land I would consider calling the pound.

Y NS N   21. If I have a choice I'd rather be indoors than outdoors.

Y NS N 22. Living in the country is very similar to taking a vacation in the country.

Y NS N 23. I have a good idea of how much land to purchase for the purposes I have in mind.

Y NS N 24. I don't mind having a job or business in which I may have to wear many hats.

Y NS N 25. I enjoy having friends and neighbors stop by and chat at odd hours.

Did that survey put you through some changes? Good! It's never too early to begin contrasting what you *think* are the good and bad things about the country versus what they really are (for you). The following answers bode well for your move to the country: 1/n, 2/y, 3/y, 4/y, 5/y, 6/n, 7/n, 8/n, 9/y, 10/y,11/y, 12/y, 13/n, 14/n, 15/y, 16/y, 17/y, 18/y, 19/y, 20/n, 21/n, 22/n, 23/y, 24/y, 25/y.

We're not going to explain why certain answers are "right" or not; finish this book and you'll understand why. If you got every one right, go to the head of the class . . . and prepare to move to the country! Missed five or so? Better read this book thoroughly and stop skimming! Missed ten or more? Maybe you're not suited to living "beyond the sidewalks," as J. D. Belanger writes in his *Countryside* magazine. On the other hand, you may find you're fairly suited to a small city or town in a rural area—just not trying to be the ultimate back-to-the-lander, let's say. The author started in small cities like Eugene, Oregon, and, over time, "worked down." That may be what you'll do, too.

Chapter 2

Planning for Your New Beginning

If you've decided to "take the plunge," the first thing you need is a plan. Sure, I've heard of people who have quit their city jobs one day and stuffed a station wagon full of possessions the next. Day three found them in a small town and, just possibly, day four with a new position. But most of us can't move that fast—nor would we want to. There are just too many loose ends that might come back to haunt us.

Most of the clients of the Greener Pastures Institute have an informal two- to three-year timeline to consummate a move. Some plan to do it in a few months, others take up to ten years. I tell those who don't have a plan that you need to have a beginning and an end or it just won't happen.

Any kind of beginning is a start. The accompanying "premove checklist" will give you some ideas of things you really *have* to do. (Obviously, No. 1 is "develop time frame.")

Also obviously, your plan will be different from others'. Couples with jobs and children in school may have the hardest time organizing a move. Retirees who have just sold their home have little to constrain them except the acquisition of a moving van.

People come to GPI at various stages, from the exploratory stage to the verge of embarking on a research trip. Most come because they value our insights into the process and, in particular, want our inside information on locations.

Of course it's possible to move without a plan, but wouldn't you rather play it safe and have one? I know of no human endeavor that isn't enhanced by a little foresight, and moving involves a total lifestyle change. Better to be prepared.

JUMP-STARTING YOUR MOVE: 15 STEPS YOU CAN TAKE NOW!

Getting a move off the ground and out of the "fantasy" realm requires, first, a willingness to commit to a time frame (one to ten years?) and then to start taking actual steps toward the move's culmination.

Lots of us get stuck in both places.

To help you stay focused, here's a "premove checklist" you can use to create a sort of flowchart.

❑   Determine a reasonable time frame. (The "average" is two to three years, but what if you're not average? Could you move quicker if events (earthquake, riot, etc.) precipitated it? Would a job offer or a sudden house purchase offer be factors? Now try to work it out on paper.

❑   Discuss your prospective move with family and friends. What are the pros and cons? Even though many may not go along with you (literally and figuratively), at least you've cleared the air.

❑   Determine your "relocation readiness."

❑   Develop a "manageable" (5–10 maximum) list of prospective locations. Perhaps start with states and winnow down your list to towns within them.

❏ Write to chambers of commerce and other agencies for data on towns which are prospects. Ask for the relocation, not "tourist," information. Addresses can be obtained through the *Worldwide Chamber Directory* available in your local library.

❏ Subscribe to the local newspapers in the towns you're interested in. You can probably learn more about towns this way than any other way short of visiting! Get addresses from chamber packet or from a *Gale Directory* in your local library.

❏ Obtain local phone books of the areas in which you're interested.

❏ Take the first of several investigative trips (both winter and summer!) to the communities you're considering. Talk to as many different types of people you can to really find out how locals view their towns. Attend town council meetings, meet the newspaper editor, attend church, etc.

❏ If you need to job hunt, try to line up interviews in advance of your visit. This is difficult to do but possible if you go about it the right way. You must send individual cover letters to employers specifying the exact dates you will be in town, and then follow up with phone calls. Get major employers from *Walker's Manual to Western Corporations* (available in libraries) or *Standard & Poor's Directory*.

❏ Interview several real estate brokers/agents in your "finalist" (two-three?) towns. Choose the one who can represent you best (he or she will have access to the Multiple Listing Service and can represent any property in the data). Place a "real estate wanted" ad in the local paper to ferret out for-sale-by-owner (fsbo) properties where you may be able to deal directly with owners. But strongly con-

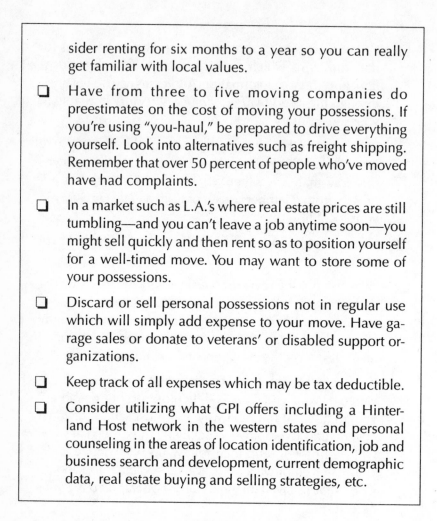

sider renting for six months to a year so you can really get familiar with local values.

❑ Have from three to five moving companies do preestimates on the cost of moving your possessions. If you're using "you-haul," be prepared to drive everything yourself. Look into alternatives such as freight shipping. Remember that over 50 percent of people who've moved have had complaints.

❑ In a market such as L.A.'s where real estate prices are still tumbling—and you can't leave a job anytime soon—you might sell quickly and then rent so as to position yourself for a well-timed move. You may want to store some of your possessions.

❑ Discard or sell personal possessions not in regular use which will simply add expense to your move. Have garage sales or donate to veterans' or disabled support organizations.

❑ Keep track of all expenses which may be tax deductible.

❑ Consider utilizing what GPI offers including a Hinterland Host network in the western states and personal counseling in the areas of location identification, job and business search and development, current demographic data, real estate buying and selling strategies, etc.

YOUR FINANCIAL EXPECTATIONS

Our financial expectations of a new place are all different. Most of us recognize that in "trading down" to a smaller place we will make less money—if making money is even an issue. As a rough rule of thumb, I estimate that you will make about 25 percent less in salary moving to a small city of 50,000 to 300,000 and 50 percent less moving to a smaller town of less than 50,000 population.

These figures depend, of course, on a variety of factors—such as what field you're in and how the local economy is doing.

Over the years I've seen more and more programs develop to help people get a grip on the financial aspects of moving to a smaller place. (This is obviously a new field because, in the past, it was always smaller to bigger, as if there were some inherent value in greater size.) The Right Choice program in Massachusetts is one (wish I'd thought of it myself!). Right Choice goes beyond salary—which can be the same in different parts of the country and you *still* haven't a solid idea of whether variations in local living expenses will support your lifestyle or not. Right Choice computations compare your projected salary with local expenses via a computer model: everything from motor vehicle insurance to heating bills, local taxes, cost of food, etc. The fee is about $200.

We've referred quite a few customers to Right Choice over the years and haven't had any complaints. The analyses are not cheap, but if you are considering buying a house in a new town and know pretty much what your salary will be, it's the way to go. The reasoning is sound. Why go somewhere where you know your standard of living will decline when it doesn't have to?

On the other hand, a lot of us simply can't predict what we're going to be doing when we get to our personal Edens. I have advised many clients not to buy houses until after a substantial waiting period. Many are determined to move to a place that doesn't necessarily have great financial promise, at least in the short term. There was no Right Choice to guide my wife and me in choosing Bend, Oregon, in the early 80s. In fact, I was rather hardheadedly in favor of it for some of the wrong reasons.

Another factor is that many of us plan to go into business for ourselves, and I doubt if even buying into one of the bigger franchises can assure you of a particular income stream. If you buy a going concern you may not know that the company books have been "massaged" (nice word for "altered to pull the wool over your eyes").

The truth is, if I hadn't made the mistakes leading up to starting a relocation service, I probably wouldn't be dispensing advice today. Had I used a Right Choice (not that I would necessarily have had the money or the assurance of a job), I would probably be doing something very different today. In other words, moving to greener pastures is always a bit of a crapshoot, a roll of the dice, a leap of faith.

But the book you're reading being from a financial publisher, well, I have a certain obligation to give you the best financial information I can!

Besides Right Choice, the American Chamber of Commerce Research Association (ACCRA) is a useful tool to compare the cost of living in about 250 locations throughout the United States. A magazine called *Where To Retire* in Houston, Texas, regularly summarizes some 100 of them.

What ACCRA does is keep track of costs and then report on how much you will have to pay to live, say, in Pueblo, Colorado, versus San Francisco. That could be up to 50 percent, though most of the time it's 10 to 25 percent. What ACCRA doesn't reveal, of course, is that the *big* nut—housing—may vary up to 75 percent or more. *And* that there are all sorts of ways you can stretch a dollar. For example, rather than pay the utilities their "average" to heat your home, you can use wood or insulate heavily and use passive solar. More on housing options later.

Other sources of cost comparisons are the local chambers of commerce, your own surveys when you visit places, local newspapers, data obtained on-line, GPI's Hinterland Hosts and such excellent reference books as the *Places Rated Almanac,* updated every four years (or its software equivalent from Fast Forward, Inc.); *Location Guides*; and *Rating Guide to Life in America's Small Cities. Places Rated Almanac* can't be beat for comprehensiveness in one big encyclopedic book, but appreciate the fact that the statistics and interpretations are based on Metropolitan Statistical Areas (MSAs), which generally have at least 100,000 or so people with a central city of 50,000 or so. *The Rating Guide* is specifically for cities that are just below MSA population criteria.

ADVANTAGES OF A TWO-PERSON HOUSEHOLD VERSUS A ONE-PERSON HOUSEHOLD

Can two live more cheaply than one? Probably, as a percentage of total household expenses. If you're a renter you know that you might pay $400 for a one-bedroom apartment versus $550 for a two-bedroom apartment in some cities—so at least in terms of housing, about three-quarters (72 percent) of what you are paying goes for the basic amenities, which could be shared. Even factoring in heating and electric costs, two can probably live more cheaply than one in a small apartment; the extra room won't make that much difference in the bills.

Leap a little ahead of me and imagine, then, what a group of people could do on land that is essentially group owned. That is the essence of the situation at Greener Pastures Institute today, though the amount of sharing is voluntary and one's financial responsibility for each individual land parcel is entirely one's own.

When I was counseling job seekers in Bend, Oregon, I was always happy to see couples in my office, especially if they were recent urban expatriates. I knew that a couple or group would stand a better chance of making it in a small town. It's awful when you lose a job or business but not *so* awful when you're part of a team that's still employed/employable. I generally began to conclude that it was the resourceful couples who stood the best chance of survival in a small city or town.

CORPORATE HEADQUARTERS IN THE HINTERLANDS

Most of us seem to work for corporations or the government these days. Trading a corporate job in the city for one in the country has its plusses, however, which are not well understood.

As a young person I got quite good at competing successfully for corporate jobs. I had an arsenal of well-crafted resumes, dressed well, was always willing to do an employer's bidding, etc.—until I got restless (long story). One thing I noticed, especially reading personnel journals, was that corporations were always looking for the perfect candidate (which you should always try to make yourself into) but that they had no sense of geographic loyalty. They would just as soon hire you from way across Los Angeles as next door in their very own community. It was no wonder that many of the "perfect" candidates they hired got tired of long commutes on gridlocked freeways. These same corporations would then complain about inveterate "job hoppers." (Of course, there are corporations that *raid* others' personnel.)

The big city may have many job choices, but there's lots of this kind of competition—and backstabbing. I'd like to be able to say that corporations in smaller towns have more loyalty to their employees, and vice versa. Of course, a lot of you have seen *Roger & Me*, the Michael Moore documentary on what happened when GM pulled out of Flint, Michigan. Obviously, GM had no particular loyalty to Flint, though Moore argued via a clever series of vignettes that it *should* have. But Flint is not typical because, for one thing, it was the location of just one of several GM plants.

A corporation that essentially grows up in a particular town, or which moves lock, stock and barrel to one town, does, I think, feel a greater degree of "community responsibility." An excellent and unique book on this subject is *The New Corporate Frontier* by David Heenan (see resource section). Since we live in a capitalistic society and an increasingly capitalistic world, always hedge your bets. But I feel more comfortable working for small town corporations.

You do need to know that such corporations generally hire locally long before they hire from afar—unless they are in the process of moving to a town or haven't had good results recruiting locally. Corporations that are moving to town are often announced on the front page of the local newspaper, so you have a chance to get to them before they actually relocate.

*I*mportant Tip . . .

While the choices are fewer, doing a corporate job search in a smaller city or town may result in a career opportunity less likely in the big city. Corporate employers tend to be more loyal and may have to answer to the communities they reside in. If you can wear many hats you may well have a long-term opportunity with a nationally or internationally oriented one.

Most companies expect you to work at least six months to a year before they will give you a reference if you go somewhere else. I realize that when you move to a new town your first job may simply be a stepping stone—but don't mess it up for others to follow, or we'll have the big city mentality in River City before you know it.

Corporate and government jobs represent the most secure, stable jobs in the countryside. Corporations that have national markets may be able to keep you during the typical seasonal ebbs and flows of the local economy. There are rarely layoffs in government positions—especially if they are in the area of "staff support" like clerical, accounting, computer services, etc. The worst I've seen is mandatory four-day work weeks because of a budget crunch, and most of us in Eden would just go fishing or hiking!

Getting a government job usually requires filling out reams of tedious application forms, taking qualification tests, and getting on a waiting list. I remember scoring about 96 percent on a test in Oregon to be a publications coordinator and then languishing on a list for over two years. I never did get called; apparently no one in the state was hired—probably because no one ever quit to create an opening. And knowing how hard it is to get a government job—especially in the states everyone wants to move to in the far west—might also compromise a person's new lifestyle options.

But government jobs do have lots of perks, like retirement plans, full medical benefits, sick leave, vacations, etc.

In addition to job search skills, it is helpful to have access to directories of corporations and/or government agencies that are in a position to hire you. If you are a company seeking to relocate in one of the idyllic places thousands of highly qualified workers want to live in, there's help for you, too.

INVENTORYING YOUR SKILLS AND ASSETS

At the end of the last chapter was a short quiz to help you recognize that there are certain qualities and knowledge useful to those who will be living in rural areas.

If it wasn't clear to you at the time of "testing," having the ability to do a variety of things in the home or on the job will serve you well in Green Acres. In our industrial, rather specialized society, few of us are raised to be Renaissance types—or jacks of all trades. And perhaps at this point you don't in fact know the range of things you can do. Becoming more aware of your skills, and of how they could fit into a rural setting, is a first step toward making a transition.

Between 1981 and 1986 I wrote people's resumes in Bend, Oregon—at least 5,000 or so (1,000 a year). One of the techniques professional resume writers use is the "summary of qualifications" (SOQ) statement. Many of us have a difficult time summarizing all the qualities we can apply to a prospective job. Most of the time we don't even attempt to do it. The SOQ is a good device for that.

I once wrote an article for *The Wall Street Journal*'s Business Employment Weekly about how "re-entry women" could and should make as much hay on their resumes about their past accomplishments—domestic or vocational—as possible. I stated that for many women with job gaps, there were/are experiences in their backgrounds that would qualify them for jobs if only they knew how to "package" them. For example, a leadership role with the PTA might well translate into public relations or customer relations skills—something needed by many firms today.

Of course, in the supercompetitive job market that exists today, work experience and *accomplishments* will make your resume rise to the top of the heap on a CEO's desk.

In short, you need to take stock of your skills, experiences and accomplishments if you aspire to move to a rural area. It is helpful to do that by listing everything you do well or fairly well.

You might want to put together a "functional" resume or two if you're planning a job search. The more resumes you have the better, because you'll keep your options open for applications to different kinds of jobs. The biggest mistake people make in resume writing outside of poor format and grammar is having a "generic" resume that the job seeker, lazily, hopes will be applicable to all openings. There is probably a greater need for good professional resume writers today than ever before, although I suggest you try your hand at it and run it by a professional for a "critique."

EIGHT TIPS ON EFFECTIVE RESUME WRITING

1. ***Think accuracy, brevity and clarity (the ABC's).*** Journalists invented these ABC's and you'd do well to heed their seasoned advice. Your resume should be accurate, reflecting verifiable past experiences and present qualities desirable to employers. It should be brief—*preferably one page*, two at the most (with a few exceptions). Spelling, grammar and punctuation must be perfect or very nearly so; nothing stands out more glaringly than a misspelled word or unintelligible sentence. If in doubt, consult a professional resume writer, English instructor or, in a pinch, secretarial service.

2. ***Develop a strong objective statement.*** Every resume should have an objective statement that, in one or two sentences, summarizes what you desire to and *can* do for the employer. "Seeking a challenging career position in Engineering utilizing my ten years' experience and

demonstrated success in the field." Don't bury this component—it belongs right up there at the top under name, address and phone number. Use a general statement rather than no statement at all. For example, "A challenging, responsible position with a local employer leading to career and company growth."

3. ***Accentuate abilities, training and potential skills.*** Present and/or previous employment should be described in terms of accomplishments, levels of skill and responsibility, and personal/professional growth achieved. Avoid the temptation to simply list job duties, especially if they are redundant throughout your experience history or obvious to the prospect. If you have been promoted quickly, say so. If you supervised personnel, tell how many. If you increased firm productivity or sales, use figures if convincing and not limiting to your case. Avoid puffery and self-aggrandizing language.

4. ***Choose a style that fits you.*** Two common resume formats are the *chronological* and the *functional.* Chronological resumes organize experience and education from the present to the past. Functional resumes organize according to categories of information such as type of work experience or skills. Most resumes are chronological, but functional resumes are becoming increasingly popular because they can camouflage job gaps and present qualifications more succinctly, avoiding the "list" look. Other specialized formats include the curriculum vitae and qualifications brief.

5. ***Create a graphically pleasing package.*** First impressions count. Don't discourage readership with a badly typed and reproduced document. Resumes typed with a smudgy nylon or cloth ribbon and copied onto cheap 20-lb., white bond paper have two strikes against them from the start. Typing with a carbon ribbon or word proces-

sor, or even typesetting reproduced by an offset printing process onto a higher grade of off-white paper can help your self-promotion stand out from the crowd. Typeset resumes using desktop equipment are the norm today. But don't go overboard. A factory worker's resume need not have the elegant look of the executive's.

6. ***Minimize obvious or subtle background negatives.*** Resumes are selective information and, as such, need not be exhaustive. Avoid novelization or narrative. If there are periods of unalibied unemployment in your background, eliminate reference to them if possible. Don't volunteer unfavorable information about reasons for leaving a job. Eliminate salary history—it might be held against you. If you are a woman, don't mention number of children and, if divorced, state single. As a rule of thumb, drop age if you are a woman over 40 or a man over 50.

7. ***Eliminate unnecessary personal data.*** One survey revealed that employers *are* interested in your hobbies, especially if they are sports they share an enthusiasm for, but don't list everything from A to Z. Try to zero in on interests relevant to your career orientation (such as flying, if a business exec). Eliminate any references to church or political affiliations—for obvious reasons. (Exception: state "active in church drug abuse hot line.") Such items of information as age, sex, height, weight and health are arbitrary; some states have laws prohibiting employers from using this data as a basis for hiring, anyway.

8. ***Target your market with the cover letter.*** A survey of 500 executives of major firms revealed that the cover letter accompanying your resume is as important as the resume itself. No resume sent through the mail (or electronically) should be without a personal note detailing your ability to meet the specific needs of that one company. Cover letters should be no more than three to four

paragraphs long on one sheet of matching paper. They should be typed (unless handwriting is asked for) and personally addressed if possible. Graciously ask that an interview be arranged at the employer's convenience.

Writing a resume is hard, which is why professionals are well paid to do it And since the challenges of job hunting from a distance are great, a well-written resume helps and is worth paying for.

Of course, there are some occupations for which employees—even in smaller towns—are in demand. (Most employers are more than happy to rely on the local labor pool, which often includes many ex-urbanites with specialized skills.) Health care professionals, computer programmers and salespeople (retail and direct) are examples that come to mind. But I still haven't met the rural employer who would pay you to move to his or her Valhalla. Yet this is done all the time by big city corporations who have a hard time luring professionals cross-country, especially if organizations like Right Choice (see later chapter) make it abundantly clear to their clients that the trade-offs in overall cost of living simply won't justify the increase in salary.

If sending your resume to a few dozen rural employers was all it took to get a job outside the city, there obviously wouldn't be so many people in the cities! In my own efforts to secure a job from afar, almost every employer I ever wrote to (*if* they even bothered to answer at all) said *come here* and then we'll talk. This kind of encouragement does open doors, but you could waste a lot of money following up on an interview prospect that might fail to materialize.

What I tell clients who must job search from afar is: Make it as easy for the employers to respond as possible, and make them feel special. Enclose an SASE for a reply (why should *they* have to pay the freight to respond to you?). Make sure each one gets a personal—or made-to-look-personal, word processed—letter. In the cover letter, state that you plan to move to their town by such and such a date (even if you don't); too many resumes they receive are just too vague. Tell them what you can do for them. And try to pin them down to a week when you "plan" to be in town for interviews.

---

*I*mportant Tip . . .

Make it as easy as possible for an employer to respond to your resume or application from afar. Enclose an SASE, offer to take a collect call (unless you have an 800 number), give him or her an e-mail address, etc.

It's far better to be selective than send out hundreds of impersonal, untargeted resumes. Of course, if all you want is an entry-level job (which is OK, to get your first local reference), then the scattershot method might bear some fruit.

I recommend winnowing your choices of location down to five to ten maximum. You might send out ten letters and resumes to employers in five different towns. Perhaps you'll get interview interest from two employers in one town, one in another and none in the rest. Do plan to visit the towns in which you have some leads. Once you get there you can blow in cold at some employers, fill out applications and hope to get an interview before you have to leave.

This advice will greatly increase your odds of lining up some interviews (which, I tell clients, is halfway to home base). Most jobs are "won" at the interview stage. This is a little hard for a writer type like myself to appreciate, since I'd rather put all my effort into a resume, but lots of experience has shown its validity.

I don't know how many jobs in smaller towns are advertised versus not advertised, but a job search expert in Seattle wrote in late 1994 that in today's market only about 10 percent *are* advertised. This is a sobering statistic if you've been used to just applying to ads in the help wanteds. Anyway, having a job prospect or two, if you're in your working years, tends to make a possible move a lot less anxiety provoking.

CONDUCTING AN EFFECTIVE JOB CAMPAIGN FROM AFAR

I'll be the first to admit that trying to find a job from afar is one of the toughest things you may ever have to face. Some 50 percent of all cross-country movers end up moving without a job, according to a statistic from *American Demographics* magazine. It was drummed into me early that I shouldn't, as a young person, go anywhere without a job lined up already. But the logistics of trying to job search from a distance are challenging. That's why half just give up and move.

What follows is very specific information and inspiration for prospective small town relocaters. It has been said that looking for work is harder than working itself. And when distance intervenes, "harder" becomes "hardest."

Marketing your qualifications by mail or electronically—which many relocaters are forced to do to save time and expense—may seem to the applicant to be a relatively painless way to go. But it is far less effective than applying in person for a bona fide job opening, completing the necessary company forms and getting interviewed on the spot.

Put yourself in the shoes of a small town employer (who, being human, has prejudices much like yours). Would *you* hire someone based on only a few flimsy documents sent "over the transom" from afar?

Most job offers go to people with: (1) good connections, (2) excellent qualifications and/or (3) good interviewing ability. In general, small town employers, before committing themselves to a hire, have the opportunity to look eyeball-to-eyeball across the desk at an applicant, receive verbal answers to their questions and make some physical contact (a handshake). Even in this age of cyberspace, I doubt if this is going to change much.

So, from the outset, the odds are against getting an employer's attention with only an impersonal form letter, generic resume and other supporting documents. Ask any electrician: paper is a non-conductor!

Understanding all this, it is still possible to make meaningful contact with a small town employer from a distance and receive an honest reply, not an anticlimatic "thank you for your interest, sorry there are no openings" (if you get anything at all).

Most applicants who have never had to look for a job from a distance just don't know how to do it. They of course expect much too much from their resume, don't personalize the cover letter, and often simply present themselves as quasi-literate, disorganized and even insensitive to a company's needs.

Such presentations—*unless* the applicant is in a high-demand field like nursing, accounting, auto mechanics or computer repair—in perhaps 95 percent of cases, are promptly round-filed or, with bigger firms, dead-filed.

Eaton-Swain Associates, an outplacement firm, conducted a survey revealing that a personal note or cover letter accompanying a resume is absolutely crucial to further consideration. Eaton-Swain sampled 500 executives in top U.S. companies. Most employers, Eaton-Swain learned, assume an unsolicited resume without a cover letter means the applicant is out of work and is a poor prospect. Small town employers may feel much the same, though no one, of course, has ever bothered to survey them.

This means applicants must intensify their efforts to convince employers they are not just "fishing." A well-targeted, personal note can do this if it addresses the following areas:

- Specifics of the openings—if actual—plus your qualifications and relevant experience
- Knowledge of the company (culled from an annual report, news article, trade directory, etc.)

- Suggestions on how to increase the firm's profitability *or* reduce its overhead (firms make money both ways)
- Your willingness to come to an interview at your own expense, on short notice

As previously discussed, resume approaches can differ. What is important to keep in mind is that they present verifiable, positive information while avoiding damaging negative material.

For example, an employer might want to hire a salesman because he or she "increased gross sales at Acme Corporation by 200 percent in one year." But the fact that the salesman held ten jobs in ten years (though not entirely unheard of in the sales field) would probably disqualify him or her. To fracture an old cliché, if you can't say something good about yourself in your resume or cover letter, don't say anything at all.

Another very important thing that many long-distance applicants overlook is reference letters. You can say anything you want on a resume (and employers aren't stupid), but it's only *your point of view*. When accompanying letters essentially substantiate what your resume claims, your case is stronger. (When you're new in a town, you really need reference letters.) Not that reference letters are always credible. Those written by a relative or friend simply don't stack up against the praises of a former employer, business owner acquaintance, or minister or attorney who can not only vouch for your character but may have something to lose by fudging.

Don't get discouraged if you've mailed out a few dozen resumes and haven't been offered a job. If you are getting personal letters, faxes or e-mail back indicating employers would like to interview you, consider yourself halfway (or more) to home base. Most employers narrow the interview field down to a manageable five to ten (from possibly dozens), and if you get this far, you've struck potential paydirt.

HOW MUCH ARE YOU WORTH?

Whether or not you need to job hunt or start a business, you need to know what your financial assets are. You may know them in your head, but it is still helpful to set up a personal Financial Asset and Liability sheet.

Many people count heavily on their ability to sell their home and realize a lump sum in equity. Before 1992 or so my "equity refugee" clients in the Los Angeles area (as the media portrayed them) did have money burning holes in their pockets. Los Angeles real estate values had gone up, up, up for at least 15 to 20 years without a blip. Unfortunately (and yes, we predicted it in one issue of our newsletter in 1990), property values were due to decline as much as 50 percent. Some of GPI's counseling sessions were more like therapy sessions. I'd refer people to financial planners but they still wanted to know from the "guru" what he thought would continue to happen to southern California real estate values.

Today fewer and fewer people, at least in California, can sell out and put together a grubstake that way. Many could once buy homes in rural areas outright. More and more people may be taking our advice to buy undeveloped land and build in a low-cost, alternative way.

How much will it cost to move? In the book *50 Fabulous Places To Raise a Family*, there is a detailed description of actual expenses that can total almost $50,000 (see page 38). I was shocked to see it and my tendency is to pooh-pooh it. Not everyone has to sell a house or hire a huge moving truck. This kind of figure must discourage many. Of course, there are people (some reading this book) to whom $50,000 is a relatively small amount considering the potential for a total life gain. But single people or families who rent shouldn't have to spend anywhere near that figure. So, use the form on pages 39-41 to do a rough sketch of what you own, what your debts are and how much cash you could make available for the move.

I once met a couple who had nearly $100,000 in combined income and were up to their eyeballs in debt. (Another therapy session.) They had virtually no assets, no house or savings. I told them they needed to contact Consumer Credit Counseling to help them manage their debts. They were in no position anytime soon to move. They needed to start socking money away any way they could, and there are quite a few city people like them—huge sala-

Average Cost of Relocating a Family of Four (685 miles) (based on a present home value of $137,390)

Present Home Carrying Costs (annual): $ 3,167
Mortgage interest, insurance, property taxes, utilities, repairs, maintenance, improvements and miscellaneous costs

Sale-of-Home Costs: $15,057
Resale loss, broker commission, mortgage charges, appraisals/inspections, legal costs, marketing costs, title expenses, transfer taxes, buyer incentives and miscellaneous closing costs

New Home Purchase Costs: $ 5,275
Mortgage application fee, appraisal fee, mortgage insurance, origination fee, discount points, survey fee, legal and title costs, recording and transfer fees, miscellaneous fees

Possible Interest on a Bridge Loan $ 545

Shipping Household Goods (7.7 rooms): $ 7,519
Transportation, packing and unpacking, insurance, storage and shipment of one automobile in peak season

Pre-Move Home Search Trips: $ 2,950
Two trips to destination city for family including transportation, lodging, meals, car rental, childcare, entertainment, incidentals

Temporary Living Expenses: $ 6,095
Forty-five days for one adult to rent apartment or live in a residence-inn, including lodging, meals and incidentals plus three trips to old home

Final Moving Trip to New Location: $ 578
Transportation, lodging, meals

Miscellaneous Relocation Expenses: $ 4,167
Utility hookups, cost of joining clubs, unions, a house of worship, etc.

         TOTAL   **$45,353**

Source: PHH Homequity Corp.

Assets

Cash Reserve Assets

Checking accounts/cash $ _____

Savings accounts _____

Money Market funds _____

Certificates of Deposit _____

Life insurance (cash value) _____

Equity/Retirement Assets

Time deposits (T-bills) $ _____

Stocks and options _____

Retirement savings (IRAs/Keoghs) _____

Annuities (surrender value) _____

Pensions (vested interest) _____

Profit sharing plans _____

Collectibles _____

House (market value) _____

Other real estate/limited partnerships _____

Business interests _____

Personal property (auto, jewels, etc.) _____

Loans owed you _____

Other assets _____

TOTAL Assets $ _____

Liabilities

Mortgage or rent (balance due) $ _____

Auto loan (balance due) _____

Credit cards _____

Installment loans _____

Annual tax bill _____

Business debts _____

Student loans _____

Brokerage margin loans _____

Home equity loans/2nd or 3rd mortgages _____

TOTAL Liabilities _____

TOTAL Net Worth _____

Source: *50 Fabulous Places To Raise Your Family* (Prometheus Books).

Cash Flow Analysis

Income

Husband's salary/bonus/commissions — $ _____

Wife's salary/bonus/commissions — _____

Dividends and interest — _____

Child support/alimony — _____

Annuities/pensions/Social Security — _____

Rent, royalties, fees — _____

Moonlighting/freelance work — _____

Loans being paid back to you — _____

    TOTAL Income — $ _____

Taxes

Combined income taxes — $ _____

Social Security contributions — _____

Property taxes — _____

    TOTAL Taxes — $ _____

Living Expenses

Rent or mortgage payments — $ _____

Food — _____

Clothing and uniforms — _____

Utilities — _____

Dining out — _____

Furniture/electronics — _____

Vacations/recreation — _____

Entertainment — _____

Gasoline — _____

Car payments — _____

Auto repair and maintenance — _____

Financial and legal services — _____

Medical care/medications — _____

School tuition/day care — _____

Life and disability insurance — _____

Car insurance — _____

Health insurance — _____

Cash Flow Analysis, *continued*

Property and casualty insurance   _____
Pet care   _____
Birthday and holiday gifts   _____
Babysitting/housekeeping   _____
Commutation (tolls, trains, etc.)   _____
Cable TV   _____
Household maintenance   _____
Telephone bills   _____
Religious institutions   _____
Books, magazines and papers   _____
Clubs, sports, hobbies   _____
Dues—union and others   _____
Alimony/child support   _____
Parental support/nursing home   _____
Personal allowances (kids, lottery, etc.)   _____
Other   _____

TOTAL Annual Living Expenses $ _____

Source: *50 Fabulous Places To Raise Your Family* (Prometheus Books).

ries that are frittered away on multicar payments, exorbitant rents, dining out, expensive electronic purchases and so on. I'm paid to have sympathy but I really don't have much. If they can't live more simply in the city, how are they going to do it in the country? Probably they hadn't thought that far ahead.

If you don't have equity in your house, savings or other assets you could liquidate, like stocks, coins or a business, then perhaps relatives can help. Most people start businesses with gifts from relatives (*not* with bank loans) and you may be planning to do this, only in a new setting. The time to ask for a loan or gift is obviously after you have secured a job or have leads on one, and signed a rental agreement or whatever in your new locale. But predicating a move on the *possibility* of a handout from a relative or friend is risky business which might create long-term weighty financial obligations you don't need at this juncture.

DOWNSCALING YOUR MATERIAL NEEDS BEFORE YOU MOVE

Living more simply may not be popular (although *Time* magazine made it its cover story on April 8, 1991) or stylish, but it is necessary. On the subject of living frugally in the city in preparation for doing the same in the country, what *can* you do?

This is a good subject for me and my wife, Laurel, because we really don't know any other way! As a young journalist and even small business owner (me) and child care worker and artist (her), we never made the kind of salaries many professionals do that enable all the perks of city life. But at the same time we began to realize that those higher salaries tended to perpetuate urban dependency. If you make a lot of money, the marketers descend on you like vultures. The city has dozens of TV channels, radio stations, newspapers and so on that constantly urge you to buy, buy, buy. And don't get me started on the subject of credit. . . .

We need, as individuals and as a society, to "get real." A lot of high salaries are evaporating now as corporate America eliminates what it perceives to be fat. One estimate is that some four million middle managers have gotten the axe since the late 1980s. Free trade/NAFTA means that over time we'll be creating a "level playing field"; for the *short term* this means U.S. salaries will go down while our trading partners' salaries and standard of living go up.

I don't have a problem with this because we've been spoiled far too long. World War II created unprecedented prosperity. I grew up in a middle-class home. My dad worked 25 years for Lockheed Aircraft Corporation and we always had everything we needed, including a succession of nice homes in the suburbs. (Dad was smart. Although I didn't like moving as much as we did, he would leverage the credit he had established buying one home into a new home, retaining the old one as a rental.)

This period just before the 1950s was unprecedented in its industrial output, especially in the machinery manufactured to allow us to enter World War II. The depression years conditioned us not to get caught without a job, or a paid-off house, or a food larder. So we baby boomers came away with the impression that our parents were very materialistic—which, by contrast with their own upbringing, they were indeed.

A lot of baby boomers (75 million strong) continue to believe that every generation must somehow do better financially and materially than the last. Even if many of us (as I did) consciously reject the materialism of our parents, we still have nagging insecurities about our material adequacy in a world made up of people still essentially trying to keep up with the mythical Joneses.

But since the first Earth Day In 1970 we've become acutely aware of what we humans can do to trash the earth. Again, living simpler lives may not be popular or stylish but it is *necessary*.

While still in the city you can consciously make an effort to get out of debt. Start with everything you are financing at this moment. Our society seems to be increasingly dependent on 10 to 20 percent or more interest rates we pay to have things we otherwise couldn't afford. Cars and homes are the classic examples. But have you ever asked *why* you can't afford to own them outright? That's a marketing and banking conspiracy if ever there was one. It goes like this: convince everyone they need a big fancy house that they don't even have a hand in building themselves, two cars in the garage or under the carport and other baubles of "the good life," then give them the means to buy them on credit. (Good luck when one person in a family loses a job.)

I must confess I've never owned a new car or even financed one. I thought recently that if I had the $10,000 to $15,000 in cash to buy one outright (rather than finance it), would I? My Dad has been able to do this.

And my answer is: I think not. The way cars depreciate, I could probably get a dependable used one that's two to three years old for half or less of what I would pay new. (Of course having even $5,000 in cash to buy a car these days will often strap you if you live in the city.) But Detroit wants you to think that you're un-American if you don't buy new.

Trying to buy a house outright is about as far-fetched a fantasy as any there is. But just 150 years ago, people built them with their own blood, sweat and tears—and *some* money. (But that was before the 50- by 75-foot lot—with hardly any trees you could fell or even dirt you could pound into bricks—became "standard.") Housing is really where we have missed the boat. We need to encourage a nation of owner-builders, or at least old house recyclers.

𝒥mportant Tip . . .

Think unconventionally about housing possibilities in small towns and rural areas. As we will learn later in the book, rural areas offer many choices. It may well be feasible to build your own house with a little help, or find a bargain fixer-upper that will become a gem with a little elbow grease.

In southern California's volatile real estate market I've often advised clients to sell their heavily mortgaged residence before their equity shrinks further—and go rent for awhile. Or to become apartment managers, house sitters or caretakers—steps, by the way, that might better position you to move when the time comes (or, I should say, is planned for).

Aside from the big-ticket items, consider how you waste hundreds if not thousands of dollars a year buying prepackaged food from grocery stores. A person we know is a middle-aged homemaker who cooks everything from scratch and has made sort of a science of it. She is a master (should I say mistress?) at buying in bulk and eating "lower on the food chain." You'd be surprised how much you can save by not eating meat protein as many times a week as most Americans do (you'll probably be healthier, too).

But, hey, I'm a relocation expert, not an economics expert (of course, maybe they're basically the same thing!). Since the greedy 1980s a number of newsletters and books have come out to help people downscale. You may have heard the titles of some of the newsletters: *Tightwad Gazette, Living Cheap News, Non Consumer's Digest,* and others. Some of their addresses are listed in the Resources section.

Being a penny-pincher is definitely in, whether in the city or the country.

WHERE TO GET HELP DURING THE PLANNING PERIOD

Planning a move can be a lonely job. Certain aspects are exciting, but you can't share it with just anyone. Certain family members may disapprove, especially if they think you're trying to get away from *them!* Obviously, you can't confide with most employers, many of whom will have your position filled these days at the *rumor* you may be leaving. Certain friends and neighbors may actually envy you, however. I know a lot of our clients have found warm fellowship with other prospective urban opt-outs via our classes and programs. For awhile Greener Pastures ran a Saturday support group called EMIGRANTS (Endangered Metropolitan Inhabitants and Growth opponents Relocating in Arcadian Neighborhoods, Towns and Suburbs). It was an opportunity for people to share their dreams and their nightmares about the process, vent about city living and pick the brains of yours truly.

You should certainly consider hiring professionals to talk to who can help smooth the way to a transition. Many family therapists are sincere and skilled. Financial planners are increasingly adding relocation issues to their stable of services. Real estate professionals may have contacts in the town you plan to move to who can talk to you about their location. More about them later.

GPI has been developing a list of Hinterland Hosts, people willing to talk or write to you about their transitions, their towns and so on. Many are ex-urbanites and former clients who have successfully relocated. We're very excited about this two-year-old project (although it's been hard to keep going).

Making peace with family, friends and all manner of soon-to-be-exes is challenging. Many will say, "Oh, Johnny (or Susan), you can't possibly move away from your friends/relatives. And what about the good job you'll be leaving?" That's just to make sure you feel like you're jumping off the edge of the earth.

Maybe you'll get a more receptive response, like this: "Oh wow, Johnny/Susan! I've always wanted to escape the rat race like you plan to do. Take me with you! No, I guess I can't go. I sure hope you won't forget me!"

Leaving the people in your life behind is bound to be painful, although some of us may turn out to be relieved! But clearly going to a new place will put much stress on you in terms of making new acquaintances, as we discussed in Chapter 1.

We've had clients who serve as "advance persons" for their whole families. Occasionally, Greener Pastures Institute has had *several* families or sets of friends in our very small office trying to work things out together. Usually, though, it's a couple who doesn't have a whole lot to lose in terms of relatives or friends in a move. It may be that a friend or relative has already moved to the place the client is considering—which, unfortunately, ends up being some town in a state that everyone *else* is moving to (a "mecca"). But we feel that makes it a whole lot easier emotionally and possibly financially.

Incidentally, the author and his wife and one-year-old moved to Bend, Oregon, in 1981 knowing nobody, although we did have a friend 120 miles away who came over the mountain pass to look for property for us. When we say we knew *nobody* that wasn't quite right. We had been corresponding with the president of a church we were interested in joining. That correspondence eventually resulted in an offer to "squat" for two weeks in the president's duplex while he was away on sabbatical in San Francisco! That helped us tremendously. Bend was in the premecca stage when we moved to it; now there's even a TV show about it!

Obviously, the more concrete you can be about your future plans the easier it will be for relatives and friends to accept. Securing a job first, as we indicated before, may be unrealistic though possible if you go about it correctly. Having housing, as we did at least short-term, was a plus. We also had ideas about businesses we wanted to go into and some capital (not enough, as it turned out).

STRATEGIES FOR PRODUCTIVE RESEARCH

We'll cover this in more detail in the next chapter, but here are a few tips. As we'll discuss, the problem in trying to determine if a new location is right for you boils down to time and money. The ideal is to be able to spend at least a few months both winter and summer in your prospective Eden and not rely on a lot of indirect, supposedly objective and blatantly subjective dispatches by authors, chamber of commerce officials and even people like me. But urban people are generally busy, and vacations are getting shorter.

The indirect method can at least be fun, especially insofar as it helps you winnow your choices to just the places you want to visit. That's probably the No. 1 thing clients want us to do, so we've developed some very graphic materials that make it possible to talk about a lot of places in general, as well as some in detail. Right now we have a color-coded map of the western United States which overlays town size, and multiple smaller U.S. maps that detail information like where nuclear power plants are, where growth is occurring, where radical fringe groups hang out, what the climate zones are and so on. We are hoping to acquire software that will allow us to do a while-you-wait printout of statistical details about the towns that look like good prospects. As yet, however, this software hasn't been developed for anything but Metropolitan Statistical Areas (MSA's), or areas above 50,000 or so population, and on MS DOS format.

Basically, you can do this research yourself from the comfort of your living room or a good library (though finding some of the little-known relocation/quality-of-life books may be challenging). A lot of people get immersed in reading and researching while they're awaiting "direct action." Trying to winnow your list of possible Shangri-La's from all the books and publications out there these days will keep you busy in your spare time *and* keep you pumped up. I'm amazed how many people are willing to subscribe to a newsletter but unwilling to buy some of the books recommended, most of which are in GPI's catalog. The average customer spends less than $20 on us or books, yet is willing to give a real estate agent and moving van company thousands—and they're not very concerned with your success where you're going. Quite frankly, it is little wonder so many people move and fail— they simply don't do enough homework.

Having a pile of books, reports, pamphlets (and possibly software in your computer) at least will give you a good feeling that you're covering as many bases as possible. If I were contemplating a serious move, I would invest a minimum of $100 to $200 in research materials—but it all depends on your budget.

Having a pile of good stuff to sift through can become a fascinating hobby for weekends or weeknights. I've often thought that trying to pick the perfect place to move to should be a board game, and there has been discussion about one. Couples could play it using the materials at hand—maps, charts, graphs and so on. One player might know something about a place the other doesn't, or a question would come up whose answer needs to be looked up, and so forth. I don't know what goes on behind the closed doors of other people's homes; as a relocation expert, I have always had some very unusual inside information to guide my wife and me (and an office set up specifically for pursuing this "hobby").

Chapter 3

Assessing Entrepreneurial Opportunities in Small Town America

I'm bullish on going into business even knowing what I know about your chances of survival—which, depending on who you talk to, may be good or not so good.

It is probably true, according to the Small Business Administration, that within five years 80 percent of all businesses are kaput.

What this so-called universal statistic doesn't tell us is that many businesses change their names and locations, which probably makes them difficult to account for with any statistical methodology. Some new businesses may well be half-hearted efforts that die a well-deserved early death. Other businesses may be sold. Of course, there are a lot of "underground" businesses—especially in rural areas where the government doesn't have as many snoopers—which simply never get detected and so cannot be evaluated. The point is, a lot of businesses survive in one form or another.

I happen to believe that going into business today has been made unnecessarily complicated. I read in *Inc.* magazine that young people especially are being discriminated against because of the complicated rules and regulations of federal, state, county and city governments. They, in today's economy, may be having the hardest time of all.

Many of us simply don't have the resources to fully set up a business (if that is the route we plan to take versus buying or franchising—more on those subjects later) on the chance that it will be successful. I've always started the five or so businesses I've run on a veritable shoestring. Where I put my money first—rather than on business license fees, expensive stationery, a rented office or a company car—is in *testing an idea*.

When we moved to Bend, Oregon, in 1981 we came prepared to start three different businesses: a carpet steam-cleaning operation, a copy service/secretarial service, and a graphics/typesetting business. We had some basic equipment from a previously successful business in southern California and had recently purchased a photocopier. (The copier cost $1,000 and turned out to be a poor investment at that. I don't remember what motivated me to buy it before arriving in Bend, and normally I wouldn't advise you to invest in equipment/machinery before testing the waters.)

My decision to pursue at least one of three businesses was based on some preliminary research, which included a scan of the competition in the yellow pages, chats with a few of my potential competitors and faith that the local economy would rebound from the recession of 1979-1983.

After running ads for awhile for my carpet steam cleaning business, I found that there was simply too much competition for that. I lacked the equipment to go into it as more than a sideline.

Nor did I have the equipment to run a full typesetting/graphics operation, but I was probably right in thinking I could open an office and "subcontract" jobs to other typesetters for awhile until I acquired the equipment or went in with someone else. And I found a good location—right next to the DMV in a small mall—which encouraged me to strike while the iron was hot. The Bend Words & Graphics Center was born.

A few months later I was almost exclusively writing and reproducing resumes for people because as the recession deepened that was what people needed. (Fortunately, I had once worked a short time for a franchise in Los Angeles that did resume preparation.) I kept the name Words & Graphics Center later when I closed the office and moved in with a personnel agency. In an odd sort of way it still represented what I was doing!

I wrote resumes for about five years and in the early years sometimes had a land sales business. I was the only professional resume writer within a hundred miles. A competitor sprung up a couple of years later next to the chamber of commerce, lasted about a year, and went kaput.

I admit I got lucky in being able to start and persist with a business that I never intended to run in the first place, but you can see that I was, initially, quite serious about going into business, was determined to find something that worked and, fortunately, had cash reserves to last about six months (a year would have been better). I was also able to find part-time work to supplement the business's down months.

Probably what you need most in starting a business is a *good idea.* An idea may evolve out of personal interests you have, a previous business you've been in, knowledge about a particular field, a connection with someone you know who's already in business, or research into the latest start-up trends. I can't tell you exactly where to start because I don't know you.

You need to ascertain as soon as possible where you plan to start a business and then become as familiar as possible with the terrain. One suggestion is to spend a few days in your small town of choice asking residents what businesses or services they would like to see established. People do indeed have opinions about such things! I also attempted to get a letter to the editor of the local paper printed on this subject so that suggestions could be made initially without a research trip.

---

*I*mportant Tip

One point about going into business if you've never been: You may have read long lists of "qualities" you should have before going into business, such as resourcefulness, a willingness to work 12-hour days, perseverance, organizational skills, a business education, marketing ability and so on. All these are of course important, but *motivation to succeed* is the bottom line.

You can learn about business by just getting out there and doing it. I was no expert resume writer when I started, but I perceived a need and I had the confidence that I could somehow meet it. Four years later I started the first national association of professional resume writers from Bend, Oregon.

There are a lot of reasons why businesses "fail," but *failure* is a relative term. No one wants to fail but often it takes a few failures to achieve success. Even a part-time business may be perceived a failure in the world of full-time businesses, but it may be just the ticket for you while you're working for others, trying to build it up. I'm at the point in my life where I simply don't think in terms of individual successes or failures but rather overall progress on a life and career path. That, despite a setback that saw our business nearly fail in one recent year, keeps me (and my business activities) going forward.

With what I know about business today, I wouldn't want any business that wasn't home-based. Retail businesses pin you down to set hours. Anybody can walk in and steal your money. If you lease or rent a location, the landlord can raise the rent and/or kick you out. But maybe this is the kind of business you want to be in. Watch out for large, discount chain stores, though. One of these may be the death knell for your little niche retail business on Main Street.

What has been called the Bible of the home-based business movement is *Working from Home (Everything You Need To Know About Living and Working Under the Same Roof)*, by our friends Paul and Sarah Edwards (Tarcher/Putnam). This 550-page "encyclopedia," which lists Greener Pastures on page 15 in the latest printing, embraces "new locations," is updated frequently and is now in its fourth edition. There is inspiration and information galore from a couple who point out that nearly 32 million Americans work from home today—up from about 8 million a decade ago. A survey of the readers of Greener Pastures' newsletter revealed that 81 percent would like eventually to work part-time from their home. Obviously, GPI's customers recognize that to be successful in a rural area the likelihood of having to run some kind of business are great (but presumably also desirable).

Beating the drum for corporations to make it more possible for people to work out of their homes for some very good reasons (higher productivity, less commuting time and cost, more lifestyle flexibility, etc.) are a few telecommuting pioneers like Gil Gordon. Gordon runs seminars nationwide attended by firms like AT&T and American Express which are rapidly becoming "sold" on telecommuting. It's not exactly self-employment but it can feel a lot like it! Gordon sees the possibilities for rural/remote areas. One thing holding rural telecommuters back is the absence of high-quality phone lines in some country locales. Faxes and modems get better results over the newer fiber-optic cables and most rural systems are copper. An article recently appeared in the *Oregonian* on how La Grande, Oregon, is trying to attract corporations willing to develop telecommuting programs, and at least one national conference has been held to develop this option.

Certainly more dynamic at this point is the activity of those brave and forward-thinking individuals who are setting up rural home-based businesses using the latest technology, which allows them to communicate nationally or even internationally. They have been called "lone eagles" and infopreneurs, and certainly this is the direction many folks are going. With a computer plus a modem, the Internet, fax, cellular telephone, solar power and Federal Express, you can probably operate some businesses from just about anywhere.

How do people who hardly ever see their customers even get paid? Well, GPI has existed for years primarily from checks mailed to us. It's difficult to obtain for home-based businesses, but you can get merchant card status to take MC/Visa payments. Another approach is called Checks by Phone in which you take a customer's bank account number and it is processed into a check via an intermediary; the check is then deposited in your bank. The latest is that three major companies have figured out how to let you sell goods via the Internet. Special coding/transcripting will allow you to send an MC/Visa account number via the information superhighway and not have it used for illegal purposes. As a business person, however, getting an MC/Visa merchant card account is extremely difficult, especially if you are in mail order.

Now onto the subject of *buying* an existing business. Is that a safer bet than starting one from scratch?

That depends, of course, on you, the kind of business, its standing in the community and so on. In general, it makes sense to purchase a business that obviously has a good track record. Being in the same location on Main Street for 50 years might be one such indication. If profits have soured in recent years because older workers have become uncreative, this might be the ticket for a turnaround.

I've never bought a business but it's done all the time. Even small towns may have people who specialize in business brokering, although the likelihood is that it will be part of the offerings of a general real estate company. Businesses for sale are listed in the newspaper. You may be able to find a business this way but remember that once you deal with intermediaries you will have less control over the outcome.

I suggest you come to town with an open mind and try to ferret out the "hidden" opportunities in the time you have. Many businesses will never be advertised because their owners fear competition or gossip. I once read that virtually *every* business is for sale—it just depends on the price! Of course, some people would be very reluctant to part with their businesses because they are more than a livelihood—they are a life.

But businesses likely to be for sale at the price *you* want are firms that, as we suggested earlier, have lost their competitive edge over a few generations, have had recent financial setbacks, are only "hobby" businesses like some we've seen on Main Street that probably never matched the expectations of their owners.

You can hear about businesses for sale by hanging out in the local bar or coffee shop, advertising for same under the Real Estate Wanted section of the local newspaper, dropping in on a chamber of commerce social, or simply canvassing the downtown and getting nosy. You may have an idea of the kind of business you want to buy, so your canvassing could be targeted.

I wouldn't walk into an enterprise with a placard announcing I wanted a business. I'd try to get to know the owner and eventually inquire how his or her business is doing. (Country firms are a lot more candid than city firms, as a rule.) You may find out that he or she has a business for sale that no one even knows about; lots of people *want* to sell things but never get around to advertising.

---

*I*mportant Tip

You never know what business might be for sale in a smaller city or town—the principals may be afraid to advertise or haven't had a good offer lately! If you get a little chummy you might find out you can buy yourself a job on fairly good terms.

Service businesses may be harder to track down, especially if the principals are working out of their homes. You may be able to do a precanvassing via the telephone (using the Yellow Pages). I'm not sure if I'd investigate businesses that advertised only on bulletin boards or in the service directory of the local newspaper; they may be just getting started.

Before buying a business, have an independent accounting firm take a look at the books. You can't take a business for a spin around the block like you can a car, although working out a "lease option" plan whereby you work in the business for a few months might be a possibility. Much depends on what the owner(s) say about the good or bad fortunes of the business. It is possible to run a business for years, barely making a profit but deducting enough living-related expenses to make it viable. There are all kinds of businesses serving all kinds of purposes—not just the big Fortune 500 ones in search of shareholder dividends and escalating annual profits.

I was impressed with the thoroughness of the Frank Kirkpatrick book, listed in the Resources section, on how to start and run a country business. The *Whole Work Catalog* is an excellent resource for those who want an overview of the many books written on specific kinds of businesses, many of them viable in country settings (like running a bed and breakfast, many people's fantasy—see next chapter). The American Entrepreneur's Association, publisher of *Entrepreneur* magazine, has several hundred business start-up manuals, many with accompanying software.

WHAT ABOUT A FRANCHISE?

The franchise organizations like to promote the fact that if you buy one you'll be better off than if you start a business from scratch or buy a going independent concern.

According to the Federal Trade Commission, there are two myths about franchising:

Myth No. 1: Franchises are safe because they have a much lower annual failure rate than independent businesses.
Reality: Economists believe the failure rate isn't so low, and some say it's roughly the same for independents, about 30 percent (first-year figures, most likely).
Myth No. 2: You have the best chance of being successful with a franchiser poised to go nationwide.

Reality: While a start-up can earn a lot of money, the risk of failure is high. Some operators sell the latest fads and then disappear.

On the other hand, Matthew R. Shay of the International Franchise Association in *Smart Money* magazine, writes that almost every study of franchising success rates conducted by such organizations as the U.S. Department of Commerce, Gallup, Horvath International and Arthur Andersen & Company concludes that franchises are more successful than independent start-ups.

For example, a 1991 study by Arthur Andersen concluded that nearly 97 percent of all franchise corporations founded in the previous five years were still in business, and 86 percent of the actual franchise stores were still in business. In contrast, a study by the U.S. Small Business Administration from 1978 to 1988 revealed that 62 percent of all new businesses were dissolved within the first six years of operation.

My personal prejudice against franchises is only that you're basically working for a corporation and may have to give up anywhere from 2 percent to 10 percent of your profits to them. Still, the risks may be well worth it if you are willing to conform to a corporation's mandates in certain areas.

On the cautionary side, I remember the news article about a well-known muffler franchise in Bend, Oregon, that appeared to be going bust. Recriminations between the franchisor and franchisee were flying back and forth at a great rate. The franchisee claimed the franchise wasn't backing them up enough with managerial and technical support. He might also have accused the franchise of poor judgment in selling the location, which had plenty of competition from independent operations already (locals will tend to keep going to places that have earned their trust). The franchisor accused the franchisee of lacking management and marketing ability and so on.

Here was an example of a big-name franchise stumbling and falling (quickly, I might add), for a lot of reasons. But certainly buying a franchise can give you a significant leg up if you've never been in business before and the profits from the sale of your house in the Big City are burning a hole in your pocket. I believe there are brokers who specialize in helping you purchase a franchise (not just their favorites) all over the country. There are a number of franchise directories which should list them. I'd certainly have a good look at all the possibilities and then start to pare down the list.

Restaurant franchises are, of course, the most visible. In the town I live near the first McDonald's just went in. In fact, it was the first franchise of any kind in this town of 3,500. Having a McDonald's in town was perceived by many to be a curse. (It certainly was to the hamburger joint next door, which went out of business but left a sign up, "Done in by a Big Mac Attack.") This kind of social stigma in a very small town may be difficult to live with, even if you *do* make a lot of money. Restaurant franchises are 24-hour-a-day enterprises, also, so be prepared for it. (In general, restaurants, we've heard, have the highest failure rates of all businesses, although I don't know the rate with franchised ones.) You need lots of employees and they'll quit on you all the time, not to mention the shortage of good ones.

Many folks favor buying into a service business-type franchise since that's where the U.S. economy is going. A few thousand dollars in technical information, training and equipment is probably recoupable, even if you have to sell the business without any "blue sky" later. Lots of businesses turn over several times in rural areas because there are a steady stream of prospective buyers from Gotham City.

Before you go into any kind of business, look around for the local offices of SCORE (Service Corps of Retired Executives). They often operate out of small town chambers of commerce or regional SBA offices. SCORE counselors are very knowledgeable and well-meaning people who want you to succeed in business. (But they get tired of people coming at them who just want grants or loans.) They can help you find financing, set up a business plan, learn how to market yourself and your business, jump through the legal hoops and so on. They will also evaluate an idea you may have. Best of all, they're totally free.

Although being in business is the most challenging work there is, it lends itself to the goals and lifestyles you may have in downscaling to a small town/rural environment. Most of us who have lived and worked in big cities are ready for the flexibility that being self-employed can give us. Of course, "flexibility" is not to be confused with the ability to walk away from a business whenever you want and go skiing! (But knowing that you can *sometimes* do it is psychologically liberating.)

There are ways to contract or expand a business to suit an individual that few jobs and job descriptions allow for. Most businesses can survive a recession, for example, if they are not debt heavy, or their owners aren't afraid to let employees or private contractors go when necessary. You do have to be willing to be chief cook and bottle washer at times.

I also think that being in business is compatible with the kind of values those who want to move to small towns desire to embrace; it is an extension of the pioneering spirit, which, I believe, is sorely lacking in America today. Many of us stay stuck in big cities because we are, frankly, spoiled by the amenities that make it possible to live narcissistically while ignoring social problems that abound within earshot.

RURAL BUSINESS: GIVING IT YOUR BEST SHOT

According to the National Federation of Independent Business, 43 percent of people get their business ideas from prior jobs. This may not be the best place, however.

If you have a business idea in mind that stems from a current or previous employer, you might ask yourself these questions: (1) does it satisfy a fundamental need? (2) does it revolve around natural resources? (3) is it needed because of an area's remoteness? and (4) would it be practical no matter how remotely situated?

These questions come from David Birch of Cognetics, Inc., author of *Job Creation in America*, who says that satisfying them will give you the best shot at a successful country business.

Another useful tool is the test called The Self-Directed Search (available from Psychological Assessment Resources, 1-800-331-TEST), recommended by Richard Nelson Bolles, author of the best-selling career book *What Color Is Your Parachute?* This test may reveal hidden interests that can lead you closer to a successful business idea.

Be cautious about taking on a business that appeals to you but which may, in the process of running it, kill your interest in it over time. The coin collector who opens a coin shop must want to live and breathe questions about numismatics eight hours or more a day—questions that are asked over and over by novices and "looky lous."

People with culinary abilities are often tempted to start an eatery—frequently a big mistake. What they enjoyed as a hobby becomes a full-time business with headaches you wouldn't believe—unruly customers, health inspections and regulations, staff that quits, cutthroat competition, . . . you name it.

A major thing I have done right in business is developing markets for services (specialty publishing, resume writing and later relocation counseling) that I didn't know a great deal about when I began—a form of on-the-job learning. I used skills I knew I had (compiling data, counseling/social work, writing/editing and public relations) to "leverage" myself into fields that have had long-term fascination for me.

I must admit, however, that I eventually tired of writing resumes and selling advertising to support my publishing ventures. In ten years of doing relocation counseling I have yet to tire of the possibilities, although the hardest part of running this business is November through February, when "the fish ain't bitin'."

𝓘mportant Tip

Some believe that if you do what you love, the money will follow. That's a little idealistic in my view, though it has worked for me to a large extent. Certainly don't go into a business in which you may tire of the day-to-day responsibilities and challenges after a few short months. First apprentice to someone who can show you real-world conditions.

EXAMPLES OF EX-URBANITES RUNNING COUNTRY BUSINESSES

In the February 1991 issue of *Home Office Computing* magazine, executive search recruiter David G. Jensen wrote about entrepreneurs like himself who had gravitated to the Sedona, Arizona, area. Sedona, of course, is a New Age "mecca" attractive to many who believe it is one of the most magical and mystical places in America, if not on the planet.

Ron and Buff Burns were running a graphic design firm, RBD Inc., in Los Angeles when the 1987 Whittier earthquake struck. (I remember the earthquake well. My son had just started elementary school in Sierra Madre; although there was little damage to his school, classes were canceled that day. It was the worst shaking I had ever experienced.) The Burns' 3,000-square-foot offices were partially leveled and they and their 12 employees retreated to the Burns' home.

In addition to the obstacles facing them in moving to a new location, the Burnses had been getting fed up with pollution and traffic. A relative suggested a vacation in Sedona, and three months later they had started commuting from Los Angeles to work there. Then they bought five acres and made Sedona their main office (they still have clients in Los Angeles).

Jensen also wrote about Tarila and Harry Turner, proprietors of First Editions, a home-based enterprise that provides marketing services for New Age businesses. (They have a nationwide directory of New Age businesses, which the Greener Pastures Institute has been listed in, as well as mailing lists for sale of natural food stores, New Age newspapers, etc.) The Tarilas, like the Burnses, are also Los Angeles refugees.

The Tarilas run a high-tech company in which all their books and publications are desktop-published in a relatively small space. Yet they reach out to a national and increasingly international market. David Jensen himself is a refugee from Cleveland via Tucson. He previously worked in management for a Japanese electronics company and was vice president of sales for a small record company. But he wanted to give up the commute, the frustrations of a job that didn't challenge him, and the mounting problems associated with a densely populated area. (His wife wanted a warmer climate.)

Jensen admits it would have been easier to move an existing business and that next time he'd do more planning. But his executive and scientific search firm is doing well. There are also many who have failed in Sedona running yogurt shops or restaurants.

I am familiar with another executive search firm that moved its medical clientele from Nashville, Tennessee, to Bend, Oregon, in the mid-80s. Obviously this kind of business isn't site specific.

I greatly admire my first cousin Eric Almquist who, as a young man, left the San Francisco Bay area, using a small inheritance to purchase a few acres in a small valley near Blue Lake, California, about ten miles north of Arcata, California. He was shrewd enough to recognize that he was partially "buying a job," as the acreage had three dilapidated rentals, which he set about fixing up.

Initially he was a potter and then later began building custom looms for the many weavers and craftspeople in this onetime countercultural enclave of California's coastal rain forest. Loom making led to other kinds of building activities (he started bartering for labor and materials with which to build two custom houses on his land). Eventually he recognized a great need by local cabinetmakers, woodworkers and other builders for specialty hardwoods (like teak, mahogany, cherrywood, etc.) and began milling and importing them from all over the world. Today he runs a very successful operation from a truly backwoods locale.

Judie and Dick St. Onge are former restaurateurs who left Orange County, California, for the then somewhat sleepy town of Arroyo Grande, California, near California's fabled Pismo Beach. Their desktop publishing and typesetting business, Word Tech, has survived for seven years, though the ups and downs of the local (and California) economy have been challenging. Judie is particularly proud of the fact that she lives and works out of her home on a main commercial strip—much like the old general store in which the family lived on a second floor and could run down the stairs on a moment's notice to take care of customers. She's just written an article on the subject for a small business magazine.

Their business has always had a steady stream of cash paying customers. The greatest challenge has been keeping expensive computer equipment up and running, and acquiring state-of-the-art technology. Dick has worked as a cab driver for years and has been developing a vending route to supplement their income which, like that of many country businesses, has ebbs and flows.

One of the most alluring businesses to prospective urban optouts is managing a country inn or bed and breakfast. But the number of country inns soared from 1,000 to at least 12,000 during the 1980s, according to the Professional Association of Innkeepers International. And this increase occurred despite the fact that the average inn of five to eight rooms loses money.

An article in the April 15, 1992 issue of *Smart Money* profiled a couple in their mid-40s, Richard and Trish Sherman (name changed), who decided to get off the fast track in sales with the IBM Corporation and purchase an 18th-century frame house outside picturesque Andover, Vermont. The article was titled "Tale from Dropout Hell," so you probably have an inkling of what's coming next.

The Shermans had money to burn, and they set about doing exactly that. The house, which had never been used for a B&B

before, needed extensive repairs that eventually added over $300,000 to the original price of $310,000. They had in no way anticipated the work needing to be done but had savings to contribute and eventually took out two mortgages (easy to obtain in the high-flying 80s).

It's a long, sordid story. They did make a success of the inn in a certain sense (grossing as much as $50,000 a year), but another $50,000 in interest payments per year and $30,000 in annual expenses were wiping out the profits. Both tired of the around-the-clock routine of cleaning, cooking, marketing, entertaining and bill paying. Clearly the Shermans were in over their heads, compensated only by an initial grubstake and their relative youth.

A couple we know, Beverly and Len F. de Geus, were instrumental in the early 80s in inspiring me to start publishing a newsletter on moving to small towns. They themselves published a newsletter for nearly ten years profiling towns, called *Small Town USA*. They're ex-southern Californians.

The de Geuses have a somewhat rosier story to tell about the B&B they started about two years ago in their home in Ridgecrest, California, out in the Mojave desert. Not laboring under double mortgages as the Shermans were (their house was paid for), they had a contractor add an 1100-square-foot, two-story addition onto their existing residence. Local officials were cooperative because the neighborhood was already zoned commercial/professional, and the chamber of commerce was pleased to be able to tell visitors in a traditionally non-touristy area about the de Geus's classy abode.

Business has been steady (if erratic), and the de Geuses report that they are meeting all expenses and are close to turning a profit. They remain very positive about the experience. They also supplement their income from Len's sideline of clock repair, which he says is often sorely needed in small towns. (In most places it wouldn't be a full-time income, however.) Len charges $85 to repair mantle and wall clocks; he repairs electric clocks as well but shies away from them. A typical job of dismantling, cleaning, polishing, repairing and reassembling takes around six hours and he hasn't had to advertise for three years to keep his workbench full.

The de Geuses, in their 60s, are great examples of active "retirees" who find that being in business is as comfortable for them as wearing an old shoe.

Rohn and Jeri Engh left the Big City to start a homebased business called Photo Source International, a photo agency on a farm in Osceola, Wisconsin. In actuality they don't supply photos directly, but rather publish a newsletter that has 1,600 subscribers among freelance photojournalists around the country. Their publication is a "hot sheet" of market tips supplied by publishers always on the lookout for the perfect image. Unlike most newsletters, however, the Enghs send theirs out electronically (e-mail) as well as via USPS so that the data stays fresh.

When the *National Business Employment Weekly,* published by *The Wall Street Journal,* interviewed the Greener Pastures Institute for a story, "Run to the Woods," it also profiled a couple in Washington State who decided that the education they were getting wasn't leading anywhere. Two years ago Dayle Massey was earning a Ph.D. in space plasma physics and his wife, Amy, an M.S. in library science. Their mutual love of the outdoors led them to think they'd rather live away from metropolitan Seattle. But how would they make a living? The answer came when someone ran an ad in the Darrington, Washington, newspaper for a broom-making company. The owners of the Traditional Broom Company had been nursing the business along for ten years but wanted to go into organic farming.

The broom company has potential, and the Eddie Bauer Company has started to sell their wares in its catalog. Their business was recently named Darrington Small Business of the Year.

Amy Massey still commutes to a part-time job as a law librarian and both she and Dayle admit that a lot of financial juggling is still necessary. But they seem to be on a fairly fast track to success.

*I*mportant Tip

Starting a business in a small town·may require that you go at it while holding down a part-time or even a full-time job or two. Businesses often evolve over time; although it's best to have a plan, remain flexible.

We know many folks running their own cottage businesses. Most are ex-urbanites. A fellow from Houston runs a bookkeeping service for small business owners. An ex-southern Californian restores old buildings and rents them out to newcomers (there is an extreme housing shortage here).

An ex-San Franciscan makes handsome decorative wooden "boxes" that are actually secret hiding places for valuables. A couple puts on seminars on how to live more sustainably: build structures with alternative materials, do organic gardening, use solar technology and so on. Another fellow operates an excavating service. A couple produces technical materials for medical organizations nationwide. Former Hawaiians own a downtown cafe. Most want to have a cottage industry but are in various stages of development with it. One woman we know is trying to develop a greeting card business using Indian illustrations applied by rubber stamp.

There are many more examples of "penturban" (areas 10 to 25 miles past the suburbs) businesses, and the information superhighway will be making more and more possible in the very near future.

If there is a common thread that runs through many of these examples it is that getting started in business is often a trial-and-error process. Those of us who have worked at "regular jobs" for years may bridle at the thought of untethering ourselves in an unknown sea. Not having an eight-to-five schedule may even be frightening, just as it can be for retirees facing days and weeks of possibly idle hours for the first time.

But idleness is rarely a problem for small town entrepreneurs. Creative thinkers (which I like to think I myself am) almost always have a new plan, and the day-to-day logistics of running even a shoestring enterprise can be daunting. Since sales and marketing are a key to the success of an enterprise that might otherwise fail (but not because it is inherently unviable), you could easily schedule an eight-hour day doing just that. Telephoning, making personal sales calls, and sending direct mail pieces or press releases to prospects is a big job, especially if you are doing it yourself or with only one other person. If you don't like doing some of that, better stick to a conventional job.

---

*I*mportant Tip

The main thing is to be willing to go with the flow and not doubt yourself. Self-doubt crops up often in the early stages when a business is barely more than a twinkle in your eye. You must also be willing to do whatever is needed to keep income flowing because in small towns and rural areas the choices are considerably fewer.

While starting a resume-writing business the author worked at various times as a janitor, ad salesman, layout artist and cab dispatcher. In the Big City he wouldn't have bothered to work at such jobs but in a country setting you may have to come down a few pegs.

It's important to review the resources in the previous chapter that can help you get ideas for businesses you may want to do.

I believe there has never been a better time in modern America to start a business—and to succeed in it well outside the city limits. I predict that not only cottage entrepreneuring but also what Marilyn and Tom Ross call "countrypreneuring" will continue to be where the career action is in the foreseeable future.

Chapter 4

Finding Your
Personal Eden

How many millions of us dream of the day when we can kiss the Big City goodbye and relocate to a little piece of God's country?

And God's country seems to be what most of us envision—a sort of heaven on earth (verdant pastures, rolling hills, pristine lakes and streams). These images, at least, came up in a survey of what people felt the afterlife must be like. (For the *good* people, I suppose.)

Actually, people's preferences for terrain seem to run the gamut from coasts to deserts to mountains. In the author's case, he's fantasized about living in all three at different times of the year. That's not a bad idea if you want to avoid weather extremes, because there is really no place in America except possibly the overpopulated southern California coast where during one part of the year it isn't too cold, too hot, too dry or too humid for some person's taste. Most of us like the climate around 60 to 70 degrees and sunny, but of course there are exceptions.

Weather and terrain are big factors, naturally, in a person's quest for the ideal personal Eden. But to be more scientific about it, we polled several hundred readers of GPI's newsletter in 1993. The question was: What do you, as an urban dweller, want some place else? The answers, remarkably, fell into ten neat categories, and almost every category had an equal number of responses. They were, in order of number of responses (but with several ties): open space, fair/low housing prices, good educational opportunities, job/career choices, environmental quality, low crime/ safety, good climate, friendly people, low cost of living and high quality of life.

Money magazine annually does a survey of the most livable cities in the United States based on such factors as health care, crime, the economy, housing, education, transit, leisure, weather and the arts. Their readers have identified and ranked even more criteria—about 50 factors for Eden; look for the annual report in the September or October issue.

Money's rankings of "What You Want a City to Offer" are headed by clean water and low crime rate (9.0 mean score) followed by clean air, many doctors and availability of hospitals (8.5); strong state government, low cost of medical care, low income taxes (8.0); low property taxes, housing appreciation, recession insulation, inexpensive cost of living, strong local income growth, future job growth, low sales taxes, cheap car insurance, good public schools, and conservationists' rating (7.5).

I think most of us are seeking a balance in a new place to live. I've often thought about that crucial moment in the life of an urbanite when the balance scales seem to tip in favor of relocating; the negatives in the Big City simply start to outweigh the positives. This is, of course, happening more and more in our urban areas today. For example, a good job, safe suburban neighborhood and reasonable climate start to lose their attraction when the company starts to downsize, gangs start to scrawl graffiti on downtown buildings and the jet stream starts to shift northward. These shifts, I believe, are what start many people thinking about moving (one of every urbanite's favorite fantasies), even if they never act on their urges.

Of course the balance is different for everybody. The annual *Places Rated Almanac* gives you an opportunity to list your preferences for a new place in a sort of stock market style chart, showing peaks and valleys. If members of your family can all do it they, can use it as a sort of template to compare and discuss the similarities and differences in weather preferences, housing priorities, health and medical needs and so on.

Money, of course, affects your choices greatly. Readers might think that I, as a relocation expert, can blithely live anywhere I want. I've had several addresses since the start of the Greener Pastures Institute, and people pay a lot of attention to where they are. The inspiration for this business was Eugene, Oregon, where, in the early to mid-1970s, I discovered I had, quite by accident, picked what the Midwest Research Institute deemed the most livable midsized city in the United States. I still have regrets about leaving Eugene, but at the time I just couldn't make a good enough living there. (Also, I dislike incessant rain.) Economics has affected my other choices as well: Bend, Oregon; Sierra Madre, California; Pahrump, Nevada; and Goldendale, Washington. As an entrepreneur whose income fluctuates wildly, I've had to find places where living costs were very low.

Our last move was precipitated by an inability to find land at a reasonable price within a sensible (and safe) distance of my client base in the Los Angeles area. If I'm born again to do this work, I hope it's with a fatter bank account.

The rich and famous may be able to travel to and live just about anywhere they want. But for the rest of us, choosing an ideal location will be based on very mundane factors like job availability/business opportunity in balance with other perceived desirables in the quality of life spectrum. How to prioritize those desirables will be discussed next.

HOW POPULATION SIZE AFFECTS LIVABILITY

In my wanderings I began to see some years ago that finding that elusive balance had a lot to do with the population size and density of our communities. And it became clear that some cities were simply too large to function effectively (garbage piled up, transportation broke down, etc.) while some small towns lacked very basic amenities like a place to go to work or a Laundromat!

Did anyone have a grip on what the "ideal" size of a community might be for those seeking a balance of family life, job choice, environmental quality, cultural amenities, health facilities and so on?

In a sense I found some examples of balanced communities early on. Eugene, Oregon, then population 70,000, was being widely praised in the early 1970s for its urban amenities yet bucolic environs. I attended the University of Iowa as an undergraduate journalism student in the late 1960s; Iowa City, set amid cornfields, was nonetheless an intellectual and employment magnet. The population was then 40,000.

Various studies began to reveal to me that communities in the 45,000 to 150,000 population range set amid cornfields, deserts, beaches or forests were often highly ranked by various straw polls and surveys of livability. Many of the *Money* magazine top cities annually turned out to be midsized, though curiously the authors didn't pay much attention to that. I certainly did.

The Zero Population Growth (ZPG) organization has produced both an Environmental Stress Index and a Child Stress Index of America's communities. In the latter study the top three cities for children were rural and under 200,000 population and the worst three were over 2 million population. I often refer to this study when parents are looking for a community in which they can raise their children safely and have a sane lifestyle themselves.

Clients often sense that cities of 75,000 to 150,000 population might be good alternatives for them. They are often very specific about their criteria. Our challenge is to find the midsized cities that everyone else hasn't already found (although sometimes that's what they want).

The problem in America, and the world, is keeping a lid on population growth. When a place is "discovered"—or has innate development possibilities—eventually it becomes overpopulated. Only a few cities nationwide have strong antigrowth ordinances in which they limit housing starts, sewer connections and so on. (I have my own ideas on how they can do this without infringing on people's freedom to migrate.) Not only do most cities and towns not have a "population policy," but the states and the Federal government don't either.

I advise you to seek places that have built-in buffers against population growth and its excesses. Why are large metropolitan areas so difficult to live in? In most cases their individual communities have "grown into" each other like a spreading gangrene. I believe we need a clear sense of where our community's borders begin and end. And preferably, we should spend most of our time within them. In Los Angeles, for example, people often live in one town, work in another, and visit relatives in still other communities. Little wonder our loyalties are so divided, and time so fragmented and scarce.

In the town I grew up in, Pasadena, there are of course many amenities as cities go: the Rose Bowl and Rose Parade, mountains close by, some beautiful museums and gardens and so on. Its population size of 125,000 inhabitants would seem to make it ideal. But Pasadena is now sandwiched between many other communities, and "border disputes" are common. There is controversy about running a freeway extension through the city (in urban areas transportation planners often mandate that individual towns compromise for the sake of the whole metro). Smog produced downwind floats lazily into town and there's no smog police to tell it to stop and stay at the city limits. If a barrio gang decides to go cruising, well, why not hit Pasadena's richer neighborhoods? You get the picture.

Take Pasadena out to a rural area somewhere where there's, say, 5 to 25 miles of distance between it and the next nearest city and you have a formula for livability.

This buffer zone of livability, or greenbelt, is beginning to be recognized as simply essential, and efforts are underway by various conservation groups to privately buy up open space that may otherwise fall under developers' backhoes. Unfortunately, it takes perspective—and money—for all this to happen and in many cases it's just too late.

There's another reason to look for communities with buffer zones: in most cases open space is devoted to some form of agriculture.

*I*mportant Tip

The best places overall in America today are midsized set, in rural or recreational counties with a "buffer zone" of open space between them and the next cities/towns. (But if you move to them, please fight to keep them that way.)

I have a problem living in dense cities whose citizens are so "sophisticated" they don't know or care where their food supply comes from. In a true national emergency, as in the earthquake that shook the residents of Kobe, Japan, recently, most urban dwellers are virtually powerless. I understand that for days Kobe residents were reduced to eating one rice ball a day, and water was extremely scarce. In a rural area you have a better chance of surviving, especially if you have room to grow some of your own food or know farmers from whom you can easily buy food.

Thomas Jefferson, in fact, envisioned an America in which the countryside was part of every city—where farms and fields were even intermingled in a checkerboard pattern within neighborhoods. My son lives in such a town in a rural part of California, where strawberry patches border housing developments. Little of America is like that anymore.

If you can afford to, I'd strongly consider moving to what F. Scott Thomas calls "micropolitan" areas, towns or cities between 15,000 and 45,000 population. His guide, *The Rating Guide to Life in America's Small Cities*, is an excellent companion to the aforementioned *Places Rated Almanac,* as is an even newer guide that covers towns in the 5,000 to 15,000 population range by Norman Crampton, *The 100 Best Small Towns in America.*

These three books (along with this one, of course) should be on any serious relocater's bookshelf. Between them nearly 600 communities in the United States are detailed and rated for various livability criteria.

If you want a regular publication that profiles towns, you might turn to a relatively new newsletter, *Small Town Search Letter*. It's quite good, profiling at least one town in the West each issue in depth. Mark Ellis edits it and it's the kind of publication the return-to-small-towns movement needs to keep the word out to disenchanted urbanites (see Resources section).

I am particularly sold on micropolitan areas because there are, indeed, communities below 45,000 population that "have it all." Bend, where I lived between 1981 and 1987, was one of the most urbane, sophisticated yet essentially countrified places I have ever encountered. It was 120 miles from the nearest urban area (rather too far, perhaps) but had everything most urbanites expect: movie theaters, malls, even high-tech companies to work at. It also had river rafting, skiing, camping and hunting. (Today, however, it's a little too "yuppified" for me.)

You may well find a micropolitan area that is poised to begin a growth curve (unless that's what you're trying to avoid). Fortunately, micropolitan areas are hard to spoil unless other micros are too close to them. They are often set out in very wide open spaces. (One reason they have so many amenities is they *have* to. Bend was the business and "cultural" center for an area spanning over 100 miles in each direction.)

Even towns of smaller population can have definite possibilities. I like to advise clients to move to the smallest town you can that still has the amenities you want. Small is beautiful. What I like about the smallest towns is the way people treat each other. In really small towns where you are likely to see your neighbors on the street all the time you can't afford to be snobby, clandestine or deceitful. In big cities you can get away with just about anything (which is why we have so many laws). Remember our reference to the study that showed that the densest, most polluted cities have the least friendly, least cooperative people? In small towns, people will bend over backward to help you out. More about that in Chapter 7.

I clipped this from a newspaper in Sisters, Oregon, some years ago. It adorns my workspace wherever I go:

"Thank God for Small Towns"

You know you're in a small town when:

- The airport runway is terraced.
- Third street is on the edge of town.
- Every sport is played on dirt.
- The editor and publisher of the newspaper carries a camera at all times.
- You don't use your turn signals because everyone knows where you are going.
- You write a check on the wrong bank and it covers for you.
- Someone asks you how you feel and listens to what you say.
- You speak to each dog by name as you pass and he wags to you.
- You can't walk for exercise because every car that passes you offers you a ride (but thanks for the offers, anyway).
- You get married and the local paper devotes a quarter page to the story.
- You drive into the ditch five miles out of town and the word gets back before you do.
- You miss Sunday at church and receive a get well card.
- A neighbor tries out a new recipe and you get a sample.
- You announce you are moving and get many offers to help.

Thank God for small towns (Sisters, in particular) and the people who live in them—and care. I'll miss you.

Moving soon to Salem,
Elizabeth A. Duncan

Well, there you have it. I hope Elizabeth wasn't too disappointed with Salem (Oregon) which, at least, is a "midsized" city and Oregon's state capital.

A word of caution: You have to earn the respect of small towners. And every place is different. It may take years before you are accepted the way someone born and raised in town is. But if you are neighborly and get involved in the community, doors will open and smiles will become an everyday common occurrence.

GETTING INSIDE INFORMATION ON PROSPECTIVE TOWNS

Getting the "straight dope" on towns you're researching isn't as easy at it might seem. If you're like most people, you can't just drop everything and do what I call a "trial move," staying in a town for two months at a time to see if it meets your expectations.

Vacation times (getting shorter every year, we hear) are simply not adequate for on-site visitations, which are extremely important. It's a good idea to visit regions of the country during winter and summer—and one vacation a year won't allow for that. Plus vacations aren't, well, designed for the "hard" work of on-site community research. It's too easy to play hooky. But later we'll address how you can make them work for you.

Ideally, you want to get your eyes and ears into a community months or years before you plan to move there. Most of us would be wise to consider five to ten towns until a few months before zeroing in on a finalist. But if we can't afford to take vacations there, we're in a genuine bind.

Chambers of commerce are the easy answer and *they* know it. They're set up to sell you on their town alone. What you get from them must be viewed through a smoked-glass filter. If you're starting a business you may want to contact the Economic Development Agency if there is one. (Bend, Oregon, was so aggressive that there were about half a dozen different agencies promoting tourism, relocation and business development.) The *Worldwide Chamber of Commerce Directory* is a good start and it's available in most libraries.

Just a word about chambers of commerce. I belonged to one for a short time as a business owner. I have nothing, essentially, against them except that from the perspective of a prospective mover you need to recognize that they are "true believers" in their communities. What they send you will often look objective (and some of the statistics are, like population size, prices of homes, etc.). But there are better sources of objective information.

𝒥mportant Tip

I have always found small town newspapers to be wonderful sources of information on towns/regions. They can tell you what locals are thinking via their letters to the editor; their editorials often reveal all sorts of things about a town; their reporters are first on the block to report news of possible employers moving in (or leaving) or toxic waste dumps being declared Superfund sites.

So it certainly behooves you to subscribe for at least six months to a small town newspaper. In a really small town it is probably a weekly. Bend, Oregon, population 17,000, had a daily, but it is more likely that towns/cities of 45,000-plus will have dailies. You can get the addresses from chambers of commerce.

Getting a phone book can prove helpful, too, especially if you want to start a business (compare the competition) or contact employers or community groups. You can order one from the directory advertising company that serves the local Bell.

GPI recently started what it calls its Hinterland Host program. Ex-subscribers to our newsletter the *Rural Property Investor* and others we trust have volunteered to help prospective newcomers to their communities via phone, mail and/or in person. This is a variation of, for example, the Good Sam recreational vehicle organization program, which publishes a directory of people all over the United States who wouldn't mind being visited by fellow travelers. That directory, by the way, is one of the best.

There are a number of "vacation exchange" programs which a book, *The Vacation Home Exchange and Hospitality Guide*, has admirably overviewed. They serve the general public or specific groups, like teachers or the military. If you have the time, you can, in effect, do a "trial move" by trading your home in one part of the country for somebody else's. It's easy because you don't have to move all your furniture (or possibly even your cars); you just do a complete switcheroo for a few weeks or a month. Call it trading places (mover style).

We earlier downplayed what you can get from the local chamber of commerce, but don't misunderstand us. Most chambers will send you a "relocation packet" (ask for it or you may get just tourist info instead). The best packets are free and contain lists of clubs and organizations, weather data, an employer contact list, economic data about the region and so on. Expect to get lots of calls and letters from real estate people who buy or otherwise acquire your name.

You may need the chamber's help only if you plan to move a business, especially one with employees. Chambers know where the industrial parks are and can put you in touch with lending organizations and building officials. Offices of SCORE (Service Corps of Retired Executives) often meet in chamber offices and are excellent (and free) sources of information on start-up financing, marketing and management in general.

PLUSES AND MINUSES OF CHOOSING THE FAVORED "MECCAS"

This section is a caveat emptor ("buyer beware") about moving to those places all your friends, relatives and others have told you about. It's not that you shouldn't consider their advice, especially if they know someone who lives there. It's just that if it's on the "map," it may be too late for you to reap certain advantages.

Our country's hinterlands were "discovered" (with apologies to Native Americans) by individualistic types willing to push westward in the face of the unknown and of potential adversity.

In my consulting business I have sensed that the twentieth century has exacted a heavy price on America's peoples: We've become soft and undaring. Many of us take the easy way out, visiting resorts and other travel destinations on our vacations and eventually choosing to relocate there because they are familiar and seemingly prosperous. Frequently all the statistical data we offer yields to an emotional decision based on familiarity and the ease of spending holiday money.

I, too, have been seduced by "meccas." Even Bend before its boom in the mid to late 80s had a reputation of being a tourist town. Skiing aficionados were saying that its ski resort, Mt. Bachelor, had powder and amenities on a par with Aspen and Vail. I knew it was only a matter of time before Bend was on the map in a big way. Recently a nationwide TV show was based on the Bend lifestyle.

Most states have a few meccas you might have heard of. In the West there's Eugene, Oregon; Boulder, Colorado; Jackson Hole, Wyoming; Moab, Utah; Santa Fe and Sedona, New Mexico; Carmel, California and others.

On livability surveys they often rank very high, especially since they have so much to offer compared with other communities their size. But statistics can be misleading.

People who really want to live in a mecca will have to "buy in." Housing prices may be double that of nearby towns of similar population size. Since many of these towns house state universities, housing competition from students can be severe. By living in Eugene six years I learned that students often feel the same way about these towns as tourists do: let's put down roots! Consequently, local employers can pay minimum wage and get M.S.'s and Ph.D.'s to line up for the available jobs. Unless you have investments or can move a business there, don't expect to survive off the wages in a mecca town.

---

*I*mportant Tip

"**M**eccas" are wonderful places if you have a lot of money, don't mind your neighbor being just like you and don't have to work at a job for a living. If you don't qualify, it may be better to pick a developing community just down the road to settle in.

Even though I was, for example, active in a Eugene neighborhood association and helped found a community center, because I could not afford property I felt like a transient at times. I did all this while going from one dead-end job to another (though I gained lots of experience). Also, early on I started a small publishing business which carried me through slack times. The irony of living in Eugene was that I actually became quite prominent and respected but still had to leave for financial reasons.

If you will be dependent on the local economy, I strongly urge you to look for a region in the first or even earlier stages of a growth curve. Jack Lessinger's book, *Penturbia*, is a useful tool in tracking counties throughout the United States that, based on 200 years of U.S. Census data, are positioned for growth (yet may also be able to preserve their quality of life). They may not be "fashionable" as yet, but being a pioneer has certain advantages. (I'm jealous of the Seavey who had a street in Springfield, Oregon, named after him—but it meant getting there in the mid-1800s.)

Penturbia incidentally, means the "fifth stage of migration." Lessinger, who holds a Ph.D. in urban planning, believes, as I do, that we have exhausted the possibilities of the fourth stage ("Little

Kingdom"), headquartered in the suburbs of some of our largest cities.

If you move to a community that's not on everyone's mecca map you may well feel like a pioneer. You will be in a position to contribute to the evolution and development of a region from the start—or possibly turn around an area that has been in decline for some time.

Incidentally, an interesting study by August St. John at New York's Long Island University reveals that most tourist-type places have built-in "destruct" genes. They tend, the study says, to follow a five-step pattern that leads from discovery to literal dissolution. Growth tends to overwhelm the very things that were the original attractions: neighborliness, a sense of community, a rural landscape, small-town atmosphere, friendliness, low cost of living and traffic. St. John's study was based on Manchester, Vermont, a 150-year-old resort village with three ski runs nearby. Many small towners are getting sophisticated about in-migration and you will certainly not always be welcomed in the "meccas."

Better that you pick a place that needs you more than you need it.

RESEARCHING YOUR PROSPECTS: VACATIONS AND RECONNAISSANCE TRIPS

As we previously stated, using vacation time to do your on-site research has built in limitations. You want to blow free after working nine to five for months on end. And you may have a limited amount of time to go to different towns.

If you're planning to move soon, I urge you to take as many holidays to conduct your research as possible. If you can line up some job interviews in a town you like on a particular day, you could fly in early in the morning and leave that night (see Chapter 4).

I suppose there are those who have moved to places they've been to only once—or not at all!—but I don't advise it. Going there twice, to experience a location in two seasons, is the bare minimum. You don't realize how many people move away from locations for one reason alone—they can't handle the weather.

If you must use vacation time, however, you might schedule a trip that will "hit" five or so communities in a region in the time you have. As you narrow your list of prospects you can plan to spend more time in individual towns on future vacations.

If you have kids, you're going to have to "corral" them for a portion of the vacation because they are simply not going to want to hang out with you during tedious trips to the chamber, to talk to the banker and so on. Depending on their ages, consider a baby-sitter or day care, a movie or dropping them off at the lake under the supervision of your most responsible teenager.

To make the best use of your time, make a "to do" list for the town (or use the one at the end of this chapter) and check things off. Don't worry, it's not going to be all drudgery! Number 1 on the list might well be to hang out in a locally owned coffee shop. Introduce yourself to some of the locals. Ask them what they like about their town and what they don't. It's amazing what you'll learn. (Big City types are often a lot more closemouthed.)

Being an entrepreneurial sort, I'm always tempted to ask locals what services they feel are missing in their town. That's a great way to get an idea of whether a business will work or not.

Another item on your list might be to attend a meeting of the town council, local environmental group or water district advisory board. You'll meet people that way and also learn things that even many locals don't know about the inner workings of their community.

Check bulletin boards. I have a theory that towns without many bulletin boards—which serve as very democratic information centers—are rather unfriendly and stuffy. You can learn much from bulletin boards, such as real estate for sale, contractors for hire at reasonable rates and so forth.

Observe how people interact with each other. Having done all the above you may already know. But stop to see how willing people are to pause and chat with each other, whether store clerks have smiles and go out of their way to help you, and if mothers and old people have no reluctance to walk freely around the town.

Talk with bankers. Will moving to their town without a job make getting a mortgage difficult? Or if you have a job already, what kind of ceiling on total house price might be imposed based on your income?

If you have children, stop by the school they might go to and chat with the principal. Ask to observe a classroom to get an idea of what's being taught and how disciplined the kids seem to be. Note whether there is adequate supervision on the playground.

Although there are pros and cons to buying a house right away (mostly cons), to get an idea of values, neighborhoods and different kinds of amenities you might want to have some real estate people show you their listings. Generally, they're more than happy to drive you around in their late model cars. There are all sorts of intangible things to look for, such as whether the police ride in patrol cars, on bicycles or on horses (if on horses, they'll be much more in touch with average citizens); whether the downtown has parking meters or the town government imposes business licenses; how restrictive the building codes are (if you plan to build or remodel a house); whether streets are free of debris and walls clear of graffiti; and whether neighborhoods have good streets and lots aren't overdeveloped.

Obviously, this is a lot to accomplish on a short vacation. Comparing notes a few days after your trip should give you enough time to let impressions sink in. If you are having trouble sorting things out, this might be the time to talk to a relocation counselor who can be the "objective third party," evaluate your research methods and conclusions and suggest where to go from there.

In some respects the research stage of finding out about prospective towns is the most fun. It must be because I've offered to do the legwork (i.e., take the trips) for clients for a fee and never had a taker. But let's face it, accomplishing the goal often leaves us with a somewhat anticlimactic feeling versus being in the thick of trying to attain it.

"*To* Do" List (Vacation)

❏ Stop by chamber of commerce

❏ Contact real estate people for tours

❏ Hang out in local coffee shop/bar

❏ Attend town council meeting or environmental group meeting

❏ Talk to local bankers

❏ Visit with principal of school/See classrooms

❏ Interview with employers (if time)

❏ Visit recreational areas and facilities

❏ Observe happiness/friendliness of locals

❏ Investigate building codes and restrictions

❏ Look at bulletin boards/advertise

❏ Go to local farmers' market or swap meet

❏ Talk with local businesses (if wanting to start one)

❏ Read local newspaper to compare prices

❏ Do something crazy—you've earned it!

*C*hapter 5

Evaluating Housing Options in Your Small Town

Most of us who have lived in the city all or most of our lives have gotten used to living in housing that seems pretty predictable: single-family homes on modest city lots, apartments, condos, maybe a manufactured home.

Moving to the country doesn't mean all this will necessarily change for the worst. For example, you probably won't be living in a cave! In fact, living in a small town or rural area can be a great opportunity to chose housing you may never have known existed.

But let's back up a bit with a little history. Ever since zoning and architectural standards began to be applied to our mostly urban areas in the early twentieth century (New York City had the first zoning ordinance in 1916), housing choices, in my opinion, have significantly diminished. It may not seem so in the number of different architectural styles there are, but those who have had the opportunity to build their own homes without government regulations and overt professional "standards" have become fewer and fewer. Government and professionals now dictate to us what materials we can use, how we can use them and how large our homes can be. Some regulation has been necessary, but after years of compounding restrictions and laws the owner-builder, once the foundation of community development, has been basically disempowered.

In short, we've traded housing flexibility and variety for housing predictability. What country living can save you the most on is the *cost* of housing because it's not tied to the urban job market. For some, living in rural areas may provide their very first opportunity to stay in one place and truly call a home their own. The author admits he didn't own a home until he began building one in 1993. He had lived in every imaginable rental known to urban areas and small towns alike, and got fed up. Some of these rentals were good deals, but after doling out over half his earnings to landlords for 25-plus years, he wised up.

Every situation is different. This chapter provides an overview of housing options in rural areas, options you may never have considered.

BUYING VERSUS RENTING IN A NEW LOCATION

This is one of the most common issues for clients of the Greener Pastures Institute, and also one that has no easy answers.

In general, I think it's a good idea not to purchase property in a new location until you've had at least three to six months to become familiar with the real estate situation. The classic scenario, which REALTORS® love to tell their peers about in small town barrooms and chamber meetings nationwide, is of the city slicker who blows into town on a vacation weekend, gets wined and dined, spots a property he or she falls in love with (aided, no doubt, by a smashing view of the mountains, friendly neighbors, a stream nearby, ducks in a pond, etc.) and plunks down earnest money right then and there.

This scene is reminiscent of the Chevy Chase movie *Funny Farm*, so check it out in the video store before you make the same mistake. (In the movie the town locals are later hired at $50 a head by the disgruntled soon-to-be-ex-owner Chase to act the "typical" role of friendly small town yokels for the benefit of a prospective new owner.)

I wouldn't recommend making a property purchase decision—one that might well affect you and your finances for the rest of your life—on the basis of a weekend trip. I also wouldn't trust real estate agents—generally paid by the seller—to show you "all that's out there." There are techniques that will widen your search immensely that we'll discuss later.

I think it's a good idea to rent for awhile. When you're actually living in your new community you will become privy to "insider" information on who's selling, become grounded in actual values and how they fluctuate depending on the time of year and other factors, and be in a much better position to work with the real estate people you choose to from close quarters rather than, say, from a few hundred miles away.

Occasionally circumstance will compel you to buy quickly. A relative or friend in your new town may have a deal for you. You may stumble on a bargain (say, by reading the small town newspaper you're receiving by mail in the city) that you know will be snapped up based on previous visits to your prospective community. You may feel pressured to roll over proceeds from the sale of your big city house into a small town estate within the two years allotted by the federal government to minimize capital gains—but remember you *do* have two years. That money could be invested in stocks or bonds, used to pay for a developing business or, of course, used to pay an inexpensive rent.

What rental? How about a small apartment with most of your personal possessions staying in storage for the later big move. It could be a small trailer or mobile home (very common in rural areas). A small house might be the ticket. To avoid rent altogether, you might look into managing an apartment (I did this once in Eugene, Oregon) or caretaking. There is a national/international newsletter for caretakers called the *Caretaker Gazette*. If you do rent, you might consider a lease option arrangement. If you've planned ahead, you may have written into the agreement a clause whereby most or all of your rent will go toward, say, a down payment on the home.

"Country" landlords often don't ask for anything more than the first month's rent plus a small security deposit (generally for breakage). Compare this with the city, where getting into even an apartment might cost you $1,500 to $2,000 in first and last months' rents, security deposits, cleaning fees, etc. Traditionally young people sought their parents' help to buy their first home; now you may need it just to rent, at least in the city.

By renting you may be able to focus on other areas that are more important in the short term than furnishing, fixing or even building a house. You may be one of the 50 percent or so who choose to look for a job after they arrive. Or maybe you need to jump-start a business. Perhaps you want to spend all your time the first few months getting to know your neighbors. Or a combination of the above.

But do yourself a favor and either buy or build a house as soon as you feel you have tested the waters, because renting long term is a dead-end street.

HOW TO SELL YOUR BIG CITY HOUSE IN SLOW ECONOMIC TIMES—AND SHOULD YOU?

We mustn't forget that for many who aspire to relocate there may be an albatross around their necks—inability to sell their property in the city. Back in 1990 we predicted in our newsletter that housing prices in Los Angeles might go down by *half*. After years of inflation, no one believed us or the prophet we got our information from. But it virtually happened. People who had bought in the late 1980s when property prices had peaked were holding expensive mortgages at high interest rates and seeing their equities shrink month by month. Some simply had to walk away from their homes to stop the bloodletting. Many people were advised to sell at virtually any reasonable price (real estate people say that *any* property will sell at the "right" price, recession or no) and rent while positioning for a move. But many were simply losing the means they had to move with—their equity dollars—and fast ceasing to be what the media had called "equity emigrants."

If the real estate market is slow in whatever city you're in, here are a few tips on how to find a buyer for your property. Right pricing is of course very important, but no one seems to get the message until they've exhausted all hope of getting the "top" price. So here goes . . .

- You might help the buyer make monthly payments—possibly for the first three years by buying down the interest rate for the period.
- You might pay for the buyer's nonrecurring closing costs.
- You could carry a second trust deed, allowing the buyer to purchase property with a low down payment.
- You could do an AITD (all-inclusive trust deed), also known as a wraparound, which is a variation on the second trust deed carryback.

I defer to real estate experts on the ins and outs of these techniques.

Some other ideas: Hire an auction company to sell your house (in the frenzy of bidding you may get more for your property than you expected in the first place).

Stage a contest and give your house away to the best essay entrant ("Why I want a home in the suburbs") who will pony up a $100 entry fee. The problem with that one is it's only through extensive advertising that you will be able to get enough entrants to realize the goal of selling your house at the price you want. (Note: This is not legal in every state, so check your state's laws before trying a contest.)

You might take the bull by the horns and leaflet a large area of your neighborhood (using kids?), broadcasting that your house is for sale. You never know—there may be someone out there who wants to add your place to his or her holdings in that particular neighborhood.

If you use a real estate agent, make sure he or she has a hot hand; ask to see a list of properties he or she has sold in the last six months in your vicinity. (Too many people list with agents they have gotten chatty with but who may not be able to do the job in tough times.)

---

*I*mportant Tip

Selling your big city house is often the big hang-up in exiting the rat race. Urban property values are going down in many of the major markets. You may have to approach this like a job search— nearly full-time. Think creatively to find a buyer at a price you can tolerate.

Should you even sell? Some urban opt-outs hold onto their properties for income and/or tax reasons or for the possibility that the move might not work out. The downside of this is that, as an absentee landlord you may have to go back and forth a few hundred miles every few months to take care of your property. If you have a regular job this may be next to impossible. It is comforting, of course, to retain ownership of a place you could return to if you had to. But there are a lot of responsibilities to contend with, and try doing an eviction from afar if your tenant refuses to pay the rent or trashes your place. Having said this, the following advice on tax sheltering may appear contradictory.

TAX CONSIDERATIONS OF A BIG CITY–TO– SMALL TOWN PURCHASE

I am not a CPA or real estate tax attorney, but this is what they will tell you about making a big city–to–small town move.

A common situation reported by real estate advice columnist Robert Bruss in one of his recent columns has to do with selling,

say, a $350,000 house in the city and purchasing a comparable—
or superior—one in a small town for $150,000. This, I might add, is
a very realistic scenario.

The difference between the sales price of the old house and
the purchase price of the new one is taxed by the government as
capital gains, and you are likely to take a very big hit. Bruss ad-
vises people to move out of their home immediately and rent it to
tenants. By becoming rental property, your home becomes eli-
gible for an IRC 1031 tax-deferred exchange of investment or business property. The law does not state what the minimum rental
period is, but CPAs suggest waiting six to twelve months before
selling the home.

The next step is to acquire one or more rental properties, preferably houses, in your new community. You want the total purchase prices for these properties to be at least equal to the sales
price of your city house.

Under a different code, IRC 1034, you have 24 months to rein-
vest the profits from the sale of your city house if you decide not
to go the rental route. But finding one that will absorb the potential profits might be challenging. I see no problem with buying
two or more homes under this rule, one of which could become a
rental (under IRC 1031) and one your personal residence. But check
with a tax attorney to be sure.

Of course, you may not want to be a landlord in your new
community, although it's a potential sideline income while you are
getting on your feet. Eventually you can sell everything, shift all
the profits into a personal residence that is *really* of your choosing,
and at least partially foil the tax collector.

By the way, if you are over age 55, $125,000 of the profits from
the sale of your city home are sheltered from capital gains under
the onetime lifetime exclusion rule. So if you have a house that's
reasonably priced at $150,000 but a slow market is preventing its
sale, a worthwhile trade-off might be to drop it down to $125,000;
you'd avoid paying any capital gains, although you'd still have to
pay a real estate agent or broker his or her commission (unless
you sell it yourself).

Another scenario involves people who must sell at a loss in the city. There are no provisions for getting a tax break in such cases *unless* you convert your property into a rental. All this gets very complicated, so you should see a CPA or tax lawyer. I don't recommend getting this kind of advice from real estate sales people or brokers.

Another tax issue you need to consider carefully is in the area of the difference in state and local taxes. According to a 1992 report by the Tax Foundation, the largest single item in a family's budget is not food or housing—but the total taxes they pay! And state and local taxes are rising at a far quicker rate than Federal taxes. The Urban Institute once did a study concluding that you pay at least *three times* more in taxes in most urban areas than you do in most small towns or rural areas. It's hard to believe, as one tax proponent wrote, that U.S. citizens pay less in taxes than any other developed nation on earth.

Anyway, moving from one state to another may noticeably affect your taxes.

How do you know which states are going to keep their taxes low? You could move to a state that isn't raising taxes because it's doing well through infusions of cash from people like you. Problem is, after the state government grants itself pay raises and remodeled offices, taxes go up.

Another issue is the kind of taxation. All states have some taxes, but a few lack sales taxes or personal income taxes. These states are well worth taking a look at (see the map on page 95 comparing state and local taxes). All states have some form of property taxation (although Alaska has no property taxes for those over 65). You can live in a state that doesn't have personal income taxes and be close to one that has no sales tax. Guess where I'd do all my shopping!

Generally, you can figure on saving up to 15 percent of your income by moving to a state that doesn't tax its citizens heavily. Also, if it is primarily a rural rather than an urban state, taxes will be lower. I would define a "rural" state as one in which there are

State and Local Taxes as Percentage of Gross Personal Income, 1991

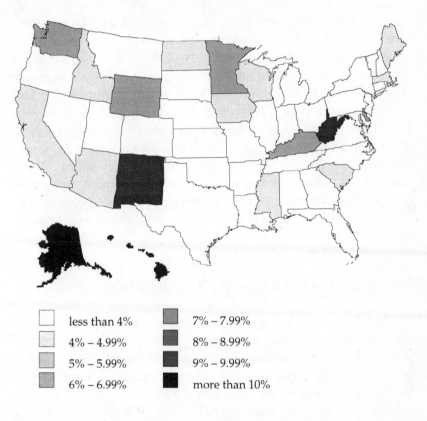

	less than 4%		7% – 7.99%
	4% – 4.99%		8% – 8.99%
	5% – 5.99%		9% – 9.99%
	6% – 6.99%		more than 10%

State	taxes	rank	State	taxes	rank	State	taxes	rank
Alabama	6.2%	18	Kentucky	8.7%	46	Nevada	6.6%	24
Alaska	15.0%	50	Louisiana	6.7%	26	Ohio	5.9%	15
Arizona	7.6%	38	Maine	7.2%	36	Oklahoma	7.8%	40
Arkansas	6.8%	27	Maryland	5.9%	14	Oregon	5.9%	13
California	7.1%	31	Mass.	7.0%	30	Penn.	5.6%	10
Colorado	4.9%	3	Michigan	6.4%	20	Rhode Isl.	6.5%	23
Connecticut	5.8%	11	Minnesota	8.3%	45	S. Carolina	7.1%	34
D.C.	16.8%	51	Mississippi	7.1%	32	S. Dakota	4.7%	2
Delaware	8.2%	44	Missouri	5.4%	6	Tennessee	5.3%	4
Florida	5.5%	8	Montana	6.5%	22	Texas	5.4%	5
Georgia	6.2%	17	N. Carolina	6.9%	28	Utah	7.2%	35
Hawaii	11.0%	49	N. Dakota	7.6%	39	Vermont	6.7%	25
Idaho	7.5%	37	N. H.	2.6%	1	Virginia	5.4%	7
Illinois	5.6%	9	N. J.	5.9%	12	W. Virginia	9.0%	47
Indiana	6.4%	21	N. M.	9.2%	48	Washington	8.2%	42
Iowa	7.1%	33	N. Y.	7.0%	29	Wisconsin	7.9%	41
Kansas	6.1%	16	Nebraska	6.3%	19	Wyoming	8.2%	43
						U.S. average	6.5%	–

only a couple of urban areas over 100,000 population. If you want to keep tabs on what states are raising, or occasionally (*very* occasionally!), lowering taxes, you might subscribe to *State Budget & Tax News* newsletter.

One final note about taxes. If you move from certain states, you may have your pension or business income taxed even if you are no longer maintaining a physical residence there. This is called source taxation. Pensions are particularly vulnerable because state governments can easily find out what you're getting, and where it's being sent. As of this writing, the following states now have laws in place that prevent your former state from seizing property if you refuse to pay: Arizona, Colorado, Nevada, Florida, Louisiana, New Hampshire, New Mexico, Texas and Washington. These laws do not mean that you will not continue to be dunned, have your credit rating affected or have a lien put on your property. Call RESIST (702-887-1296) if you want to combat this or want current updates.

WHAT KIND OF HOUSING TO LOOK FOR

We've previously discussed many of the issues related to selling your old home in the city, keeping it as a rental or immediately rolling the profits over into new property in a small town. But let's assume that you are now ready to buy or build the home of your dreams in, hopefully, the town or rural area of your dreams.

It may be that you have a good idea what you want. It may be the spitting image of what you had in the city, only less costly and on acreage or an oversized lot.

I beg you to consider a couple issues before you replicate your city home. Think of the neighbors and neighborhood. Whatever house you buy or build should be in some conformance with the standards of the area or you may find yourself ostracized. One thing locals get upset about is newcomers who immediately want to implant their urban values onto the countryside.

A lot of moves these days are toward the interior West or Midwest, where climate extremes may greatly affect your lifestyle outside as well as inside your residence. I remember my first winter in Bend, Oregon, in a kind of ranch style house that did have some similarities to structures in southern California. That winter I split eight cords of wood to keep my wife and our one-year-old son warm (I kept warm splitting all that wood). We could have used the baseboard electric heat but it would have been very expensive—and baseboard is a very inefficient way to heat anyway.

In retrospect, that house was a joke. It was badly insulated, the woodstove was inadequate and the backup heating source was poor. It was probably built by some subdivision developer from Miami Beach.

It took me a few years to wise up about housing in Central Oregon. I began thinking it would make sense to build homes partially underground, since temperatures ranged from the teens in the winter to the low 90s in the summer. The ambient temperature of the earth a foot or so below the ground generally doesn't go below 50 degrees, so you have a built-in, and free, source of insulation. Yet in six years living in Bend, I never saw a house built that way. (I'll bet the developers have wised up since then.)

I left Bend in 1987 but vowed that if I ever lived in cold country again I'd find a way to insulate so I wouldn't have to split so much wood!

It may be that you are not concerned about the cost of heating. Many Americans aren't. But high energy bills require the expenditure of precious fossil fuels like oil, natural gas and coal. Electricity generated from hydroelectric facilities is "clean" but it is capital intensive and dams up rivers. The burning of wood, which is renewable, is OK but it can cause pollution. Better that we consume less energy in the first place.

It is not surprising that many architects are now designing homes that are energy efficient, for these reasons and more. One trend is toward "off the grid" homes in rural areas. The cost of bringing power lines onto fairly remote properties may be prohibitive and people are choosing to use a combination of passive solar heating and photovoltaic (PV) electric power.

Unfortunately, it is not easy to find these kinds of dwellings for sale. They may be built by "lifers." Some banks won't loan on them for those who want to get construction costs covered. In many instances building codes actually prohibit them. Finding a subdivision of rural homes that have energy-efficiency features could be tough.

Of course, you could buy a home and retrofit it in the ways you want. Buying an older home and improving it would also be a good way to impress the neighbors with your interest in neighborhood preservation.

You will find just about every kind of housing in rural areas. Most people who live in the country, if there is any generalizing, have modest places. That isn't to say you can't have a mansion if you like. The person who can't afford a mansion in the city may well be able to afford one in a rural area because of much lower land costs, property taxes and so on. Hearst's castle comes to mind. It sits high in the hills overlooking the Pacific Ocean and is miles from even some of the smallest California coastal towns. (It amazes me that materials could even have been brought there.) The home is at least four stories high.

There are, obviously, fewer apartment houses in rural areas because the land exists to build single-family homes. There are also more mobile homes which, I understand, is the fastest-growing segment of the housing market today because it is so affordable. Even some small cities have many mobile homes. (In Yuma, Arizona, 38 percent of the housing stock is mobile or what the industry prefers to call "manufactured.") Farmhouses abound with their various outbuildings; personally, I like having enough elbowroom to spread activities under more than one roof.

There are various publications that will give you ideas about housing. I suggest *Architectural Digest* or *The Real Goods News,* which feature low-cost housing alternatives. *Old House Journal* is great if you want to restore an old place. Myriad books exist in bookstores and libraries on different housing styles and construction techniques.

It may be that you will be looking for the right acreage and find something that happens to have buildings already on it. These may be "teardowns" or they may be restorable or remodelable in some way. If you're into fairly rural living on acreage, your focus should perhaps be less on housing and more on food raising, self-employment and the natural resources that will support your lifestyle in general.

Although you may be trading down to a considerably less expensive dwelling than what you had in the city, remember that your income may well be less. A bank may be happy to lend money to you for a $75,000 property, but if you have a 30-year mortgage at 10 percent or more interest rate, you will actually end up *paying three to four times* the purchase price in compounded interest rates. Come·again? That's right. A $75,000 house could cost you $300,000 by the time you're through paying for it.

There are, of course, a few ways to soften the blow. Bimonthly mortgage prepayment strategies can help you cut down on interest payments. Adjustable-rate mortgages may save you money for a period of time. You may be able to refinance during a period of low interest rates.

But all this is still what one author called the Great American Rip Off. You're quoted a price but no one ever tells you how much it's *actually* going to cost you. Maybe you are like a lot of people in the city who figure the value of the house will just go up and up so you can always sell it to the next guy and get your equity out—but don't count on it. (Remember the Los Angeles example?) During the recession of 1979–1983, I remember hundreds of foreclosures in the Central Oregon area caused by owners who lost their jobs and couldn't keep up their mortgage payments. If they hadn't had mortgages, many could have toughed it out.

It is possible to build some homes using "alternative" materials like straw, tires and adobe for between $10,000 and $30,000. This doesn't include the land, of course. As I write, some of these techniques won't meet the building codes in many states but they are still worth considering. The codes will eventually change (but only if you insist they do). Many of us are prepared to put out up to $30,000 just for the down payment on an urban home of less than $150,000 total price (not figuring compounded interest charges), so it's a figure that's approachable. But even if you go a more conventional route you can build a fine home for between $50,000 and $100,000. Manufactured housing, which can be shipped to the site, has undergone a revolution in recent years and easily compares with stick-built structures at generally less cost. Dearborn has an excellent book on this subject (see Resources section).

One man, Bill Kaysing, has recognized that many Americans have too long been thinking castles when we might better be thinking cottages. At least many of us can afford cottages. He's built "microhouses" for as little as $900 that have all the usual amenities except lavish amounts of space (you don't necessarily need it if you have land around you). Some of his plans are available through the venerable Mother Earth News organization (see Resources section).

Housing will probably always be your greatest personal expense whether you become an owner or continue to rent. But doesn't it make good sense to make sure you have a roof over your head in good times or bad? A few years ago, in fact, I bought a small motor home to make absolutely sure I would. While still living in rentals in the city, I figured it would at least give me a quick escape option if there were a natural disaster or some uprising. At 20 feet long, it's a bit cramped for two people but I wouldn't part with "old Bessie" for anything.

At this writing, I am endeavoring to build a straw bale house on land I can pay off in a few years. Land prices are still reasonable in many places because city sidewalks haven't reached there, yet. But you can just about forget the Eastern Seaboard or coastlines of California and urbanizing parts of Oregon and Washington. The action is in the interiors. *American Demographics* magazine is an excellent source of information on where people are moving, frequently publishing color-coded maps and graphs that show migratory trends. The action is hot and heavy in parts of Idaho, Colorado, Nevada, Utah, Arizona, New Mexico and to a lesser extent Oregon, Washington and Montana at this time (see map on page 101).

A Rough Sketch of Population Growth in the 1990s

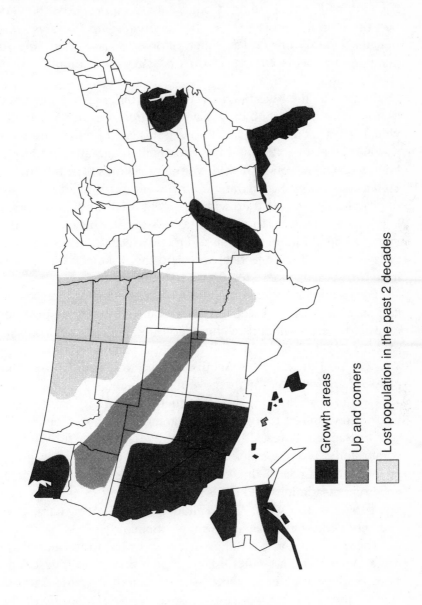

BUYING LAND IN THE COUNTRY

If you don't know anything about buying rural property, the very best book on the subject is Dearborn's *Finding and Buying Your Place in the Country* by Les Scher, attorney at law. There are so many ins and outs to it that we can't possibly cover them all here. But here are a few tips.

In general, the rules of land purchasing differ greatly from that of home ownership, and they may differ greatly even within individual states. You should also know at this juncture that you have less and less freedom, due to environmental legislation and local laws, to do what you want with your land. Writes Martin Harris in *Backwoods Home Magazine*, "Land buyers today need to be super-careful lest they end up with a parcel for which the only privilege of ownership is to pay the taxes while trying to enjoy the view." I might add that there is a direct correlation in the number of laws you will have to deal with and the distance your land is from urban areas where regulators have a foothold.

For example, if you buy land that has swamps or marshes on it, it may be declared a wetland. Even some parcels without water may be declared wetlands within a no-build buffer zone! You also want to avoid buying any land that's in a national park or in an area on the National Park Acquisition list; you could have your property appropriated by the government.

On the other hand, I do recommend looking for land which has certain built-in topographic advantages, such as being adjacent to National Forest, BLM, National Park, or Fish and Wildlife-administered lands. Otherwise you may find a subdivision going up next to your land or, worse, a toxic waste dump. (Federal government–administered lands add up to nearly 75 percent of all open space in the West. An excellent map in the February, 1993 *National Geographic* magazine shows them in detail.)

There are all sorts of things that make what to the untrained eye appears to be a beautiful landscape a poor land investment. Number one is water. If there isn't a source of water on your land—either a stream that runs most of the year, a spring, or an aquifer below the surface that you can reach to dig a well—in most cases your land will be next to worthless, especially for growing anything. (However, the very resourceful may have a way to store winter rains in cisterns, practice conservation and get by that way.)

To take advantage of the solar heating possibilities, land that is relatively flat but south-facing is preferable to land that is not.

You may be tempted to buy acreage that is predominantly sloping or in low-lying "water country" because of the diversity of natural features, even though there are only a few viable places to build structures. But consider the possibility of floods, wildfires and earthquakes that could wipe out your homestead in minutes.

Land that is too inaccessible from paved or graveled roads may become isolated in the case of the above disasters or a big snowstorm. (Make sure you know someone with a snowplow!)

The more remote your land the more costly it will be to bring utilities to it. Putting in electric or phone lines if there isn't a pole within a few hundred yards of your property may cost thousands of dollars. (Fortunately, new technologies are allowing more and more people to live in remote areas. Cellular phones, satellite TV disks and PV power are answers in many cases.)

---

*I*mportant Tip

Buying land to develop is a tricky business. There is very little good land left in the United States at affordable prices. Still, don't settle for something that doesn't "feel" right or that doesn't have the obvious necessities: a water source, growing potential, a buildable site, road access, etc.

Consider also how you will be living on the land. Most of us enjoy the companionship, at least occasionally, of others. If your land isn't within a few miles of a small town of, say, at least 3,000 people, you will have trouble getting supplies or making acquaintances with neighbors. Personally, I wouldn't want to be more than five miles from a small town or fifty miles from a midsized city of 50,000 population or more.

FINDING THE RIGHT PARCEL OF LAND

Even though no one, as Will Rogers said, is out there making any more land, there's still lots to choose from. Of course, by applying some of the above criteria it is easy to separate the wheat from the chaff (probably 90 percent of all the land that's left in the United States for sale is "chaff").

On the other hand, there is definitely a land rush going on today by eager urban opt-outs, preretirees, developers, agricultural scheme promoters and others. The longer you wait, the fewer choices you will have. There is a strong indication, confirmed recently by a story in *The Wall Street Journal*, that rural areas are due to enter a growth spurt due to a variety of factors, the information superhighway being the latest one.

There are many ways to find out about land and most of them are beyond the scope of this book. GPI's *Rural Property Investor/ Electronic Cottage Connector Newsletter* details unusual methods, like attending back-tax auctions, finding "owner unknown" land and so on. Most of you will find, however, that going through traditional channels will bear the most fruit the fastest. The more unusual methods are slower but they *will* save you a considerable amount of money.

You can, of course, call or write REALTORS® in areas that you are interested in for their listings of rural properties for sale. Often they will have whole catalogs they can send you. Chambers are more than willing to supply you with lists. United National Real Estate and Strout Realty are two national rural real estate companies with offices in many small towns across the nation. Both have thick catalogs. More about brokers later.

By subscribing to a regional newspaper you may ferret out land-for-sale opportunities not only from REALTORS® but private parties. For-sale-by-owner (FSBO) listings are definitely worth taking a look at because many land sellers will carry payments, take small down payments and so on. A good strategy is to run an ad in the Real Estate Wanted column, suggest that callers call collect and see what's out there.

The following methods we employed in 1993 could be replicated just about anywhere. Initially avoiding brokered properties, we ran real-estate-wanted ads in local papers for a number of months. In one paper we were very specific about our needs and terms (5-10 buildable acres, within 15 miles of the ocean, under $100,000, $25,000 down, owner contract). We were attempting to ferret out property owners who hadn't listed yet (or who hadn't planned to), which would allow us to deal directly and avoid a sales commission.

This was the main thrust of our "attack" on the area, which, in a different region, would certainly have born greater fruit. Unfortunately, despite the California real estate recession, this region had held its prices and its desirability, and thus the phone rang far too little. So we started cruising the region by car, looking for any kind of for sale sign on a parcel or parcels that appeared desirable. This turned out to be quite a challenge as there were easily a dozen or so small towns along with their outlying areas to cover.

I remember meeting a landscape gardener having a moving sale (but staying in the region); I offered him a finder's fee if, in the course of his business dealings, he turned up anybody selling acreage we didn't already know about. I also obtained a list of government properties in the area that were being sold due to the savings and loan fiasco. A private organization was selling a list of bank foreclosures, but feeling that most of these were likely to be single-family dwellings, I passed. (At this point we were interested only in raw land to develop from scratch.) I went to the county to find out when the next countywide back-tax auction (mostly of undeveloped land) would be held. Unfortunately, it was about a year away.

We went on an "eco home" tour of mostly owner-built houses that had conservation and environmental sustainability features, like solar power, natural landscaping, etc. We asked the owners in some cases if they knew of anyone selling. (We struck out there except for a professional architect working out of his idyllic home office on acreage, who had just completed a straw bale house; this later turned out to be our building design of choice in eastern Washington State.) Lastly, while in the area we generally tried to tell anybody we got to know personally of our interest in buying land.

OUR EXPERIENCE WITH REAL ESTATE BROKERS AND SALESPEOPLE

In the above instance we eventually fell short of our objective, but before we threw in the towel, we contacted about a dozen real estate people who we learned during our travels had land for sale. We already knew that what they had was mostly unaffordable (over $100,000 with larger down payments than we were prepared to pay) and possibly bank financed (which, despite a letter of prequalification, would be hard for us since we were in a small business). We went the extra step of offering a $500 reward on top of their commissions.

Most ignored our letter which, in retrospect, was probably not a good idea to send. Most brokers want you as an *exclusive* client. They of course *claim* that through multiple listings they can show you "everything that's out there," but I would hedge one's bets and work with several. With our letter, the brokers could not know how many other brokers would be "watering down" their efforts. Still, a very aggressive broker might have picked up on the fact that we were crying for help.

We found later that the best way to get broker interest is simply to zero in on a particular property they have and meet with them early on—being discrete about who you are and what you can afford to pay.

At this point I'd like to elaborate on why we avoided brokers in the first place which, granted, may seem like putting the cart before the horse. Price and negotiability were the primary reasons. We knew that brokered properties would all fall between certain dollar amounts, and we were trying to go below those in a private deal. We didn't want to pay a sales commission (up to 6 percent); in 99 percent of cases the broker represents the *seller,* not you, though you can pay him or her to find property for you. (We almost hired a semiretired broker to do that.)

The real estate profession, being a highly profitable one, has naturally tried to create and maintain standards so buyers and sellers alike feel they are being treated fairly. And maybe in most cases they are. But there are many other ways to look for real estate, and the purpose of this book is to make it abundantly clear that, if you want to do the still rather unconventional thing of opting out of urban society, you will need to know a few tricks the brokers don't want you to know.

No one's *really* on your side but you.

Chapter 6

Money-Saving Moving Day Strategies

The monumental day is fast approaching. After years of being stuck in the Big City, you're going to be blasting off for a new
life, "beyond the sidewalks" (as J. D. Belanger puts it in *Countryside* magazine). OK, there may be *some* sidewalks, but a lot less
crime, pollution, stress and bad architecture and freeways.

Perhaps, as suggested, you started your explorations with a
timeline—let's say four years. The last six months will find you
scrambling to make all the final connections and disconnections
necessary to make your launch. If you've ever prepared for an
extended vacation, you can figure the move toward becoming more
self-sufficient in a rural area to be like that and then some. Not
having much help in this (unless you're employed by a beneficent
corporation willing to pay your moving expenses and find you a
new home in a place of *their* choice), you'll feel it's all on your
shoulders.

Quite possibly, however, you've moved lots of times before
and at least know what's involved in packing, getting mover estimates and so on. A woman I once met who was married to a
military man wrote the consummate book about the process after

30 such moves. It was called *How To Get the "Nitty Gritties" Out of Your Move* (unfortunately now out of print). More likely, however, you haven't moved in years (the average is about five years), and even if you do remember all the details involved, there may be all sorts of new factors involved in this move.

The final six months can be a nightmare—or an opportunity for personal growth, depending on how you look at it. If you would rather look at it as an opportunity, you might consider how the people in your life will be reacting/responding. If they are encouraging and helpful, then you know they are intrinsically on your side. If an employer you can trust is intrigued by a big city–to–small town move, you may even find a job through him or her in your new place, at least temporarily. (More and more firms see the value in having telecommuting employees. Or perhaps you can open a branch office.)

You may find your friends and kin willing to do a lot to help, including putting on a garage sale, getting your house ready to sell or packing. Involving them in the process, if they have the time, may create tighter bonds and less confusion about your motives for the move. Of course, you might prefer to make a clean break for a variety of reasons and want to do it all yourself. I don't recommend it, however. This is a time when you're going to need all the help you can get.

A difficult situation is having to vacate your house quickly if it sells (which can't always be predicted). This is another good reason to rent for awhile so your move can be timed right. On the other hand, a nicely furnished, well-maintained house may sell more quickly and you may not be able to afford to keep making payments on two places.

CHOICES IN MOVING APPROACHES

Moving your possessions down the road can cost you a few hundred or even thousand dollars, depending on what approach you take. Although my experiences with movers have in general been unsatisfactory, I wouldn't want to generalize. We'll thoroughly review the moving industry later.

You might consider some creative alternatives, though. I know one person who bought a used truck for a couple thousand dollars, drove it himself, and then sold it for nearly the same amount he paid for it at his destination. I have also heard of people buying used school buses, temporarily or permanently taking out the seats, and moving that way.

The slickest move I ever made was from Los Angeles to Oregon in the early 1980s. I saw an ad in the *Los Angeles Times* advertising that an antique dealer with a big truck was willing to move people "back" to his headquarters in southern Oregon. He took a load of antiques down to Sin City to sell at inflated prices and then had to return home with an empty truck. And truckers hate "deadheading." So for about the price of a U–Haul he delivered our modest possessions, and all actually went well.

Quite frankly, I've never used a "major mover" like Bekins or Allied, though I've done business with them through the Greener Pastures Institute and thereby gathered information about their capabilities.

The reason I've never used a major moving company is simply that I never felt I had so many possessions that I needed to hire a giant truck to do it. Before I moved I often sold large items of furniture to cut down on bulk. One time I moved in a station wagon, though I had to make two 1,000-mile round trips.

Most recently I moved utilizing an independent trucking firm that promised to be reliable and "cheap." I used leverage as the CEO of Greener Pastures to get a discount and promised an endorsement in the pages of our newsletter to make sure we were treated well.

Golden Bear Movers (name changed to protect the guilty) arrived on time at our storage building, despite the fact that the main truck had broken down and all our possessions were to be hauled in one of those extra long trailers that house race cars. The driver, Big Al, looked like he might have been a race car driver himself—overweight, long hair, sunglasses, Hell's Angel type. I was reassured, however, when he said his boss "would trust him with his life." I'm not sure how I evoked that reassurance.

I paid him cash (probably inadvisable) and he promised to keep in touch via a cellular phone as we followed his route (we had a jump-start—he had to sleep off his last moving job).

The first problem was that every time we called at a pay phone to get an update on where he was (we had promised to rendez-vous at the destination within two hours of each other so as to supply help unloading) we were told by the mobile operator that he couldn't be reached or was out of his truck. We never *did* manage to reach him on the phone—and we tried a lot.

We arrived, as promised, a couple of hours after he did. And he did get there as promised, but he had dumped all our possessions on our lot exposed to all the elements (only some under cover in the storage buildings we had built). We had told him that if we were too late (we weren't) he could leave. He'd obviously left in a hurry because he forgot a valuable rented dolly, which Golden Bear never retrieved. We later found out he'd been called to another job.

There was a dispute over $100 or so that I had deducted from the cost of the move, which I probably owed Golden Bear. But considering the fact that they didn't stay in touch as promised, nor waited so we could supervise the unloading, I never paid it.

The moving industry seems ripe for exploitation of every kind. Most of our clients deserve to find a better life—considering what has happened to our cities, yet as they depart the rat race, the movers often give them a final kick in the pants.

Important Tip

Many people use rental trucks to move their possessions a few hundred or thousand miles. Rental agency policies differ, so compare them. There is increasing competition in this business; do not assume they are all alike. Shop around.

HIRING A MAJOR MOVER

Since I haven't gone this route, I can't bore or interest you with personal experiences. Until recently I thought avoiding the use of major moving companies would pay off, since what I'd heard through the grapevine wasn't positive. For example, in 1987 (latest available figures) the combined Better Business Bureaus received nearly 4,000 complaints about movers. The Interstate Commerce Commission (ICC), which regulates long-distance movers, received some 8,000 gripes. In one survey of 20,000 people who had moved, over 50 percent reported damage to items valued from $100 to $500.

It is quite true that consumers have many complaints regarding major movers. They are the butt of many a joke. If you want to see one big city–to–small town move gone completely awry, see the Chevy Chase movie *Funny Farm* on videocassette.

Part of the problem has been deregulation of the trucking industry, occurring in 1980. Before deregulation, mover costs were more standardized. Call the Interstate Commerce Commission (202-927-5520) before you hire a mover and inquire about their current standing. The usual complaints include loads that don't arrive on time, damaged furniture, surcharges and outright theft.

The big movers, of course, are very shrewd in how they deal with prospective customers. Movers stand to make huge sums off people in transition and often not in a very good position to complain or fight back. The fact is, most moves not paid for by an employer are onetime, and any business that doesn't have repeat customers is tempted to gouge and even cheat its customers.

Dealing with moving companies deserves an entire book, and fortunately there is one, by Henry Constantino, a former moving van agent. It's called *Moving? Don't Get Taken for an Expensive Ride* (see Resources section).

Below, however, are a few tips culled from a variety of sources on what you can do to protect yourself.

To get the best rates, avoid moving during the peak moving season, May 15th through September 30th. You may be able to get a much better deal when trucks are relatively idle, in November and December, for example. The difference in price is generally about 10 percent but it can go as high as 50 percent. Movers do nearly 50 percent of their business during the peak season.

If possible, contact friends or relatives who have moved recently and get feedback from them about their moving company. You might also contact reputable real estate agents, the relocation manager of your company and, of course, the Better Business Bureau.

Don't be in too big a hurry to select a mover. Take a month to two if necessary. Get estimates from three to five different firms. (Amazingly, some 60 percent of consumers get only one estimate.) You might evaluate the company that's actually moving you, not the major van line affiliated with the agent.

Make sure your possessions will stay on the original truck through to their final destination. You can well imagine what might happen if your things are off-loaded somewhere—the same kind of nightmare scenario that happens to people's airline baggage.

To determine if the mover runs a tight ship you might make a surprise visit to the place of business to determine if it is well organized and clean. Also make sure there is someone you can call to answer questions. Interstate carriers are required to give you a copy of the ICC pamphlet, "Your Rights and Responsibilities When You Move" and a copy of their most recent Annual Performance Report revealing how quickly the carrier handles claims.

There are basically three kinds of estimates: binding, nonbinding and "hybrid." A binding estimate sounds like a good thing except that the mover may inflate it, anticipating glitches down the road. Use it only if you know exactly what you're going to move. In a nonbinding estimate, your final cost will depend on shipment weight and distance traveled. Movers have been known to lowball the weight in order to get the job, according to industry experts, and others lack the experience to give good estimates. There are complaints on file with the ICC that some moves cost *double* the original estimate! Eliminate candidates whose weights are comparatively high or low.

---

*I*mportant Tip

A "hybrid" estimate—also known as a "guaranteed" or "customer benefit" estimate—allows you to pay either the binding estimate or the actual cost of the move, whichever is lower. Most of the big van lines offer this service but may not mention it unless you ask about it.

On an interstate move, you will have to have cash, money order or certified check upon arrival of the moving van (some big carriers accept credit cards and traveler's checks). If there is a dispute about charges, pay it rather than argue with an angry driver. It can, hopefully, be settled later. (You won't get your possessions until you pay it, and you could end up paying storage charges.)

Cut your expenses by avoiding unnecessary packing. In addition to the extra weight, movers charge for packing and packing boxes. They also may charge for the distance they have to haul your possessions to the truck. (There are horror stories about what happens when a big moving van can't get close to your residence; one customer living in an apartment was forced to pay $36 an hour while the van circled the block looking for a parking space for nearly an hour.)

I give my wife, Laurel, credit on this last point. We've both moved dozens of times and she suggests literally selling virtually everything you own and buying fresh in a new place rather than continually dragging everything from town to town, which tends to happen. A lot of your furniture will not fit the decor (or even the space) of your new setting, and over time you may want to get rid of it anyway.

---

*I*mportant Tip

Some of us want a fresh start. Consider discarding things that won't fit into your small town lifestyle. Especially if you are building or fixing up an old house, you will have an opportunity to redecorate to match your home's interior, style and environment.

Large items of furniture cost the most to move, so couches, refrigerators, washers and dryers, dressers and beds should possibly be sold rather than brought with you. You need to weigh the sentimental value versus the resale value and determine whether the cost of hiring a giant moving van—or even a do-it-yourself truck—is worth it.

Let's say you have a bedroom set that you're tired of anyway. On the "open market" you can get $1,000 for it, but it will cost at least $2,500 new. If you sell it, you can afford $1,500 for a new bedroom set. But if a moving van costs $2,000, you're in the hole $500 ($2,500 minus $2,000) and might be better off not using one if you don't have to.

I read somewhere that 80 percent of everything you've ever filed away will never be dealt with again. I can certainly relate to that because, being in business as well as a writer, I have half a dozen large filing cabinets plus many boxes full of papers I've been carrying around for years. The IRS requires that you keep records for only the last seven years, so you can dispose of any papers older than that. Anyway, they are fire hazards.

A word about claims. The burden of proof for loss or damage always lies with you, and recourse depends on where you live and the kind of move you're making. Some states aren't regulated and you won't be able to do much. If the state is regulated, you have nine months after the date of delivery to file a claim, and the company must acknowledge it within 30 days. They have another 120 days to pay, refuse or offer some kind of compromise.

Beginning a move and a new life may seem overwhelming if you've never done it before. It is only from doing it many times that I realize it is possible to land on your feet.

Incidentally, if you go the route of moving your own furniture, I have had *good* experiences at "both ends" hiring local labor at $10 to $15 an hour to load or unload the truck. You place an ad in the help wanted section of the local newspaper (or post one on bulletin boards) and many strong, needy individuals between regular jobs will come out of the woodwork. I've always hired them for a minimum of two hours because the work is so hard (even if the job lasts only an hour and a half, say).

Be sure to keep track of all moving-related expenses. If you are moving for job or business purposes (as the IRS phrases it) and your new workplace is at least 50 miles farther from your old home than your old home was from your old workplace, expenses can be deducted on your taxes. You need Form 3903 to figure the amount. Call 1-800-TAX-FORM (1-800-829-3676).

A clever company called Before You Move, Inc. has come up with a package called The Address Express. It's a national address change notification service that eliminates one of the headaches of moving—that of notifying magazines, membership organizations, credit card companies, friends, etc. of your new address. Call 1-800-B4U-MOVE for details. This may seem a minor point considering what was just described above, but for many people, it is a welcome service.

The following checklist is from *The Homeowner's Kit* by Robert de Heer. It is extremely useful for making sure everything runs smoothly on your moving day.

---

*M*oving Day Checklist

Last Minute Packing

❑ Check contents of drawers. Remove all spillables or breakables. Soft goods such as blankets, pillows, blouses, shirts and lingerie may be left in drawers.

❑ Pin clothing to hangers if it is to be moved in wardrobe cartons to keep it from slipping off.

❑ Remove items left in the attic or other storage areas.

❑ Empty the refrigerator and freezer so they can dry at least 24 hours before moving. Be careful not to overlook the defrost water pan. Failure to have the appliances completely dry can lead to mildew and unpleasant odor. For more information, request a free booklet, *Moving Appliances and Other Home Furnishings*, from United Van Lines.

❑ Be sure the water is emptied from your steam iron.

❑ Launder all soiled clothing prior to the day the appliance service technician is expected.

❑ Take the telephone directory with you for contacting former doctors, dentists, suppliers, etc., and for preparing holiday card lists.

❑ Pack suitcases for the trip to the new home. Put in extra clothing for emergencies.

❑ Consider packing a picnic lunch to eat while traveling. Take along snacks such as fruit and cookies for the children. Include towelettes for a quick cleanup.

Reprinted courtesy of Robert de Heer from his copyrighted book, *The Homeowner's Kit*.

❏ Arrange for a babysitter for moving day, or have older children look after the younger ones.

THE DAY BEFORE MOVING DAY

Packing

❏ If you are doing your own packing, it must be completed the day prior to loading.

❏ When household goods are professionally packed, the packing usually is done the day before the actual move. Plan to be at home during the packing process to answer questions.

❏ Be on hand when the service person arrives to prepare appliances for shipment.

❏ Point out to the packers any extra fragile items.

❏ Place a big "Do Not Load" label on any item you do not want packed.

❏ Place a "Load Last" label on cartons needed first when you arrive.

❏ In the event items of extraordinary value are to be included in the shipment, remind packers to leave open cartons containing high-value items for the van operator's inspection. Be sure you have filled in and signed the High-Value Inventory form for the packers.

❏ Take valuables with you, including stamp collections or other items of extraordinary value. Check with your local bank or post office for alternate methods of transporting valuables. Check to see if your homeowner's insurance covers valuable items after you leave your old address.

❑ Unplug all television sets 24 hours prior to moving to prevent internal damage to sets.

❑ Be sure water is emptied from your steam iron.

❑ Collect things to be packed together.

❑ Have dishes washed and dried and leave them in normal storage cabinets for packers to remove.

❑ Remove items permanently attached, such as drapery rods, towel bars, chandeliers, can openers and the like.

❑ Leave beds assembled, but disassemble water beds according to manufacturer's instructions.

❑ When the movers finish packing, be sure to sign the Certificate of Packing, verifying the number of containers they packed.

❑ Inform the police department of your move.

MOVING DAY

❑ Be on hand when the movers arrive. Otherwise, it is important to let the agent know to whom you have given authority to take your place. Be sure this person knows exactly what to do. Remember the person may be asked to sign documents obligating you to the charges.

❑ Accompany the van operator through the house inspecting and tagging each piece of furniture with an identifying number. These numbers, along with a description of your goods and their condition at the time of loading, will appear on the inventory.

❑ Be sure the condition of each item is recorded and the van operator has a clear understanding about what is to be loaded last.

❑ It is your responsibility to see that all of your goods are loaded, so remain on the premises until loading is completed. After making a final tour of the house to be sure no items have been overlooked, check and sign the inventory. Get your copy and keep it in a safe place.

❑ Approve and sign the combination Bill of Lading and Freight Bill. It states the terms and conditions under which your goods are moved and is also your receipt for the shipment. You will need to sign and date the Extraordinary (Unusual) Value Article Declaration box on the Bill of Lading, if applicable to your shipment.

❑ Check to see the van operator has the exact destination address. Be specific as to where and how you can be reached pending the arrival of your household goods.

❑ Leave the phone connected throughout the moving day. After the van leaves and you finish last-minute calls, pack your phone in one of your suitcases.

❑ Leave a note listing your new address in a conspicuous place in the house so the new occupants will be able to forward any of your mail inadvertently delivered to them.

❑ Take a last look around:
  • Water shut off?
  • Furnace shut off?
  • Air-conditioning shut off?
  • Light switches turned off?
  • All utilities arranged for disconnection?
  • Windows shut and locked?
  • Have you left anything?

❑ Lock the house and leave the keys with a responsible person or in a prearranged location.

AT DESTINATION

❑ Contact the destination agent whose name appears on the Bill of Lading as soon as possible and indicate where and how you can be reached.

❑ Make sure the house is ready for occupancy before the van arrives.

❑ If you have not already done so, contact the utility companies and make necessary arrangements for service. Ask if any of them provides free appliance connection service.

❑ Make arrangements for reinstallation of appliances.

❑ Be on hand to accept delivery of your household goods. Otherwise authorize an adult as your representative to accept delivery and pay the charges for you. Inform the agent of the person so authorized.

❑ The van operator will contact you or the destination agent 24 hours prior to expected arrival time. On the day of delivery, the van operator will attempt to contact you by phone and make an appearance at the residence if unable to reach you. If no one appears to accept the shipment within the free waiting time, the goods will be placed in storage at the owner's expense. One hour of free time is allowed at destination if the shipment is traveling less than 200 miles; two hours of free time are allowed if the shipment is traveling 200 miles or more. (No free waiting time is allowed at origin.)

❑ The van operator is obligated by law to receive payment *before* unloading the goods. Payment is required in cash, traveler's check, money order or cashier's check, unless other billing arrangements have been made in advance. Personal checks are not accepted. Payment by major credit card must be authorized with the agent of origin prior to loading.

❑ Check your household goods as they are unloaded. If there is a change in the condition of the property from that noted on the inventory at the time of loading or if any items are missing, note any damage and/or missing items on the van operator's copy of the inventory sheet. *By signing the inventory sheet, you are acknowledging receipt of all items listed.*

❑ Personally report any loss or damage to the moving company agent at destination immediately.

❑ You must file the claim yourself; the van operator cannot do it for you. Claims must be received by the moving company agent within nine months from date of delivery.

❑ To save time and confusion, place a floor plan of your new home at the entrance the movers will use, indicating where each piece of furniture should go.

❑ When unloading, each piece of furniture will be placed as you direct, including the laying of rugs and setting up of bed frames, box springs and mattresses. However, appliances and fixtures will not be installed. At your request and additional cost, the agent may arrange for this service and for refilling of water bed mattresses.

❑ To prevent possible damage, television sets, other electronic equipment and certain major appliances should not be used for 24 hours after delivery, allowing them time to adjust to room temperature.

❑ If you have paid for unpacking, you are entitled to unpacking service and removal of the cartons. If you decide to unpack at your convenience after having ordered unpacking service, remember to annotate the Bill of Lading accordingly.

Chapter 7

Hitting the Ground Running in Your New Town

Are you expecting the folks in your new small city or town to roll out the red carpet for you? Probably not if you remember the example in Chapter 1 about the couple who moved to Coeur d'Alene, Idaho, and found the environment a tad hostile to any kind of newcomer from California or "down south."

We pointed out that this was an extreme example of paranoia about newcomers—an attitude you are more likely to find in some of the United States' burgeoning "meccas." Meccas, as you may remember, are towns everyone wants to move to and where real estate prices become inflated overnight. Most of these are tourist-type towns whose chambers of commerce have pumped them up in the national or regional media to the point where, at least according to many of the locals, they don't need any more influx from outside. Meccas that come to mind include Santa Fe, New Mexico; Jackson Hole, Wyoming; Vail, Colorado; Sun Valley, Idaho; Carmel, California; and Ashland, Oregon, to name a few I'm familiar with in the West.

But if you have your heart set on a mecca there are ways you can weasel your way in. It's much more difficult and it will take longer for you to be accepted, but it's possible.

In most places a bit of foresight and discretion will help you make as smooth a transition as possible. And yes, a town may actually want and *need* you (even if they don't know it yet). Not every town or small city, just because it's in the so called idyllic countryside, has its act together. In fact, there are many towns, particularly in the Midwest and South, that are literally dying for lack of new blood.

When I appeared on the Gary Collins' *Home Show* a while back, I shared the limelight with a couple from a small midwestern town in South Dakota, along with two of GPI's own hopeful ex-urbanite clients. The *Home Show* had flown the South Dakota couple to Hollywood to tell how the town had run an ad for newcomers in the *Mother Earth News* magazine. Their town's school system needed at least one more student, they said, or it would lose its accreditation. The ad turned out to be quite successful.

Several years ago, I saw a piece in *The New York Times* about some small midwestern towns that would give away "city" lots to people willing to build and settle there. I don't know if there are other towns out there like this, but I suspect there are. We once had a call from a doctor in a small midwestern town hinting at the town's willingness to really "deal" for a few good ex-urbanite citizens. A school district in New Mexico actually advertised once for city kids and their parents to come live and go to school where crime was in short supply.

Whether the town you are eyeing is a "mecca" or not, towns everywhere need committed, involved citizens. Your money from the outside may indeed be a boon to real estate people and merchants, so you should immediately have an "in" there. Most business people treat newcomers and locals with equal respect. If you are capable of doing so, you may want to make donations to worthy local charities and civic groups (especially helpful in meccas). But my route to acceptance has generally been to get actively involved in the day-to-day or week-to-week affairs of a church, club, PTA, neighborhood association or town council. It doesn't matter where you live—volunteers are always needed, although there are generally more available in rural areas where full-time careers and commuter lifestyles are not so well entrenched. Many people find volunteering very rewarding. It's definitely the ticket to rapid acceptance.

THINGS TO DO AND NOT DO WHEN YOU ARRIVE

After you've settled in—which, depending on your time frame, may be days or weeks, we recommend that you do, and *not* do, a few things.

Things To Do

☐ Change your license plates and get local registration. This is especially important if you're moving to a place that has prejudices against out-of-staters. You may be required to do that by law within 30 days or so. Anyway, you'll feel better when you're driving around town with local plates.

☐ Get a post office box for your mail if you're going to be renting or caretaking for a while. You may end up moving several times in your new town (or even throughout the general region), and forwarding orders expire after a year. (This is especially true if you have a mail order business!)

☐ Register your children in school as soon as possible, so they can start making new friends and getting comfortable with new teachers. Obviously, it's important to try to move them at the beginning of a school year or at the midpoint, rather than toward the end of the school year.

❑ Register with the local unemployment office and any private placement firms if you're job seeking. If you haven't upgraded your resume, patronize the local professional resume-writing service if there is one. If you have the skills and need immediate cash, you might consider "temping."

❑ Check legal requirements such as business licenses, health permits, county or city taxes and so forth if you plan to start a business, etc. The most important thing you need to do (which really should have been done long before the move) is determine what kind of competition exists and set about developing a written business plan.

❑ Do make an attempt to meet your immediate neighbors soon after you move. Don't expect them to make an effort to meet you. A knock on their door at a convenient time (probably not during traditional meal times) to introduce yourself may result in a pleasant, though probably superficial, conversation. If the time you called isn't convenient, offer to call them another time to get together briefly.

❑ Do have an initial information session with a local building official to go over specific code requirements of his or her county if you're planning to build a house, either by yourself or with the help of subcontractors. Ask around about reliable contractors who can do specific jobs for you. You might want to "test" them on smaller projects before giving them a major job, like roofing your entire house.

Things Not To Do

❑ Do not go out and purchase a house right away unless you have to for tax purposes or unless you simply can't see yourself as part of the community so long as you're a "renter." And be discrete about the size and grandeur of your place. Try to buy something that fits in with the neighborhood. Locals resent newcomers who bring in outside money and show them up. If you buy in a new subdivision then it obviously doesn't matter—your neighbors will probably be newcomers themselves.

❑ Do not start spouting off to neighbors, merchants, members of the town council or the editor of the newspaper about everything that's "wrong" with the town. You'll have plenty of time to make a contribution and won't be respected if you are a "Johnny (or Joanie) come lately" determined to remake the town in the image of your former urban neighborhood.

❑ Do not make the mistake of buying everything you think you need without careful consideration of the costs involved. Recent movers are often "loaded" with cash and tempted to buy things quickly to complete the moving process. But let me tell you, prolonging the "moving process" may save you hundreds if not thousands of dollars by careful spending. This is especially relevant if you are searching for a job or endeavoring to start your own business; put the funds toward things that will *make you money* first.

❑ Do not make quick judgments about individuals you meet. Intolerance for other people's lifestyles, values and beliefs is at the very root of our problems as a society today. You simply cannot know and understand the life history that shapes a person without spending a tremendous amount of time with him or her. Drawing conclusions about what kind of people live in small towns is tough because there are truly all kinds. They include people who believe Western civilization is going to collapse tomorrow, farmers and ranchers who have lived in or near town all their lives and recent retirees seeking cheap and safe living environments. It's best to be friendly with everyone but avoid contact with those who do not seem to share your basic values or interests (life's too short).

OUR EXPERIENCE GETTING ACCLIMATED IN SMALL TOWNS

By latest count, I have lived in at least half a dozen small towns and my wife nearly the same. (Hers were mostly in the greater suburban area of Boston and mine were out in "penturbia.") Between us they have been in Iowa, Oregon, Massachusetts, Ohio, California, and, most recently, Washington state.

All this experience gives us a pretty good idea what to expect, although towns are all different and it's hard to generalize.

I went to the University of Iowa for a journalism degree, and Iowa City (then population 40,000) left me with a good impression of college towns (many baby boomers hope to retire in them for their cultural and educational amenities). As a college student you are generally just "passing through," but I can say that after two years there I feel a real sense of gratitude for what I learned. You tend to give the town "credit" because at least half its residents are connected with the University.

Two years later I was living and working in the small coastal town of San Clemente, California, trying to make it as a freelance writer/photographer. Not too successful, my first job was as a taxi driver. As your first job in a new town, I wouldn't recommend driving a taxi (except for the tips). I sent many customers on a wild-goose chase trying to get them where they wanted to go!

The lesson I learned in moving lock, stock and barrel to Eugene, Oregon (then population 70,000), in the early 1970s from Los Angeles was: make sure you have a roof over your head! A publisher friend had invited me to move there but neglected to make a proper introduction to the owner of the house I hoped to live semi-communally in. I ended up sharing a room under a used-book store with an ex-con who had a temper like Captain Hook's. (Somehow, we did become friends.)

I lived in Eugene six years, so it deserves more than passing mention. It was the first place I felt truly at home outside of my "real" home in Pasadena, California. I started a number of small businesses there and gained a reputation as a small community publisher. I used to walk in "cold" to merchants to discuss their advertising needs and we made agreements on a handshake. I later worked for the City of Eugene as a neighborhood association newsletter coordinator and for Lane Community College as a health educator in the student clinic. I still have friends in Eugene and leaving them behind was very difficult (but the rainy weather was depressing and my income was too unpredictable). Although I got off to a shaky start in Eugene, I did pretty well there for an idealistic, 20-something newcomer)

I then went back to Southern California where I eventually worked for a large Health Maintenance Organization and met my first wife. Not wanting to raise my one-year-old son in Sodom and Gomorrah, I convinced my wife that Bend, Oregon, was the next Promised Land. In all the reports I had read it was Oregon's boomingest small town, and out of the wet, overcast Willamette Valley. I was determined to live in Oregon and salve the wounds from my previous false start (if you can call it that).

My enthusiasm for Bend got the better of me, however, because we arrived about two years behind the boom. Had I checked with the state department of labor statistics I would have learned that there was a 17 percent unemployment rate at the time (1981). Not to worry, I wasn't planning to get a job, anyway. But I tried three small business ventures in about five months and was running out of capital. (One more month and we would have been kaput.) Fortunately, I got a part-time job with the City of Bend and my recently discovered resume-writing niche was starting to attract a lot of patronage from out-of-work central Oregonians.

*I*mportant Tip

A boom town can rapidly go bust depending on seasonal variations in employment, interest rates, natural disasters, the loss of a major employer and so on. Be sure to stay current on economic happenings in the region you're considering.

Essentially, we needed six months to land on our feet in Bend. Active interest in becoming a member of a local congregation secured us a free (yes, free) temporary apartment early on—from the minister himself! Housing remained a challenge, however, until we fell into managing a downtown office building in exchange for reduced rent in the attached, spacious apartment building. When the building was sold, my father bought a house we found on a quarter-acre overlooking the Three Sisters (and on a river bank), which we rented from him and proceeded to fix up. Price then: $46,500.

Bend's economy improved (it's still bustling today) but our personal fortunes remained modest. (Still, there were years in Bend when I made more money than I ever had in any big city!) We eventually left for a combination of reasons which, in retrospect, probably wouldn't have been enough to drive most people out (we weren't in debt, for example). You have to chalk it up to restlessness, I think, and the fact that I was getting tired (my wife couldn't or wouldn't work outside the business when my son entered pre-school).

Once again, it was back to Los Angeles or, specifically, Sierra Madre, a neat little town where my son Erik spent all his grammar school years and became a Little League star. I divorced and remarried (but stayed in town). The Greener Pastures Institute, nurtured in Bend, began to achieve national prominence.

The narrative that follows is a fairy tale in some ways or, depending on how you look at it, trial by fire. When it became clear that I couldn't conscionably run a rural relocation service from the "belly of the big city beast," we took major steps to "disconnect." Buying a motor home was one step and setting up the business legally in Nevada was another. We then took to the road in search of the final Eden.

Which brings us to Goldendale, Washington, which you'll read more about in the next section.

BENEFITS OF SMALL TOWN LIFE

Despite all the struggles we faced, don't think for a minute that it hasn't, on balance, been worth it. (OK, my wife has her own opinion on this). Youthful exuberance may have led me down some circuitous paths—and indeed, it may lead you down a few as well before you find your ideal place.

I don't think I've been to any small town in which I haven't been impressed with the kind of people who live there—forthright, honest, resourceful, polite, helpful, hard working. They can also be, of course, intolerant, bullheaded and chintzy. It is to their credit, however, that small city or town life *works*. In the city too many people have lost interest in making their communities decent places to live. In fairness, perhaps the problems just got away from them. But most of us know in our heart of hearts when we're being community minded and when we're not. Many people have given up trying.

You may remember the letter by a Salem, Oregon, woman, "Thank God for Small Towns." Some of the benefits, like "writing a check on the wrong bank and it covers for you," may seem a little romanticized.

But I was in the little town of Lakeview, Oregon, once, stuck there in a blizzard. I was out of cash and had only an out-of-area check written on a different bank. They cashed it for me with only a driver's license for I.D. And this was an institution, not an individual Good Samaritan.

(I remember living in New York City years ago. I needed to cash a cashier's check from a bank in Iowa. But they wouldn't cash it unless I had an account there—and then only after it had cleared the Iowa bank. This prompted a 2,000-word essay, "Banks, No Thanks!," which I still consider some of my best "indignation writing.")

My wife left her checkbook in a Goldendale store the other day and it was returned to the bank. In the city that same checkbook would probably have been stolen and forged, or tossed in some wastebasket.

In the city you're lucky if your mail gets to you if the sender gets a digit or two wrong in your street address. Yet we've received mail addressed only to Greener Pastures, Pahrump, Nevada. (Please don't do that, though.)

Goldendale is so small a town that we can count as our neighbors at Ponderosa Village the owners of a local cafe, the manager of one of the two "super" markets and the owner of a local flower shop. It's a good feeling going into a store and being known as more than just a customer—but also as a neighbor and friend.

Generally, I feel much more comfortable going up to perfect strangers and starting a conversation with them in a small town like Goldendale. I'm often surprised to find they feel the same way. I was sitting in the grandstands of the county fair watching the rodeo last summer and, being a neophyte rodeo-goer, decided to strike up a conversation with a woman next to me who looked like a typical woman rancher—cowboy boots, Western shirt, etc. She could have ridiculed my city-slicker questions about horsemanship but she didn't. Then I got bolder and asked her if she knew any farmers or ranchers who could sell me straw bales for the "straw bale house" we planned to build. The woman, who turned out to be a volunteer in the Grange cafeteria, came back the next day with a list of over 40 farmers and ranchers and their phone numbers!

While waiting to build at Ponderosa Village we have rented a small downtown apartment, so we're certainly getting to know the townsfolk. Our immediate neighbor is a widowed woman in her 70s, originally from Oklahoma. She has taken an active interest in trying to protect our cat from various neighborhood predators (including her own cats).

Our little village has community events for anyone who is an owner regardless of whether they actually live there (many own lots but, due to work or family commitments, have not been able to develop them yet).

There are potlucks, meetings of a "miracles course," video nights, summer or winter solstice celebrations, impromptu wall raisings, gardening workshops and various owners' association committee meetings. We have been fairly involved in many of them.

When we first arrived I ran over one of our cats (please no hate mail, it was an accident). We got the local vet out of church that Sunday to come into the office to look at her. He didn't seem to mind!

Lest you think Goldendale is a backward, backwoods place, several people are on the Internet and are trying to get a local access line. There is a local bulletin board, though it's underutilized as yet. The focus of most "cultural" activities seems to be the public library, where speakers on interesting topics come from all over, compliments of the National Endowment for the Arts. The other night we listened to a professor working on a book about Indians and the national parks. On other occasions there have been free music concerts.

Although Goldendale is 120 miles from the nearest big city, public radio reaches us via the FM band, so Garrison Keillor, interviews with progressive individuals and music concerts are eagerly listened to by many. A retransmitter from near The Dalles sends PBS signals (you can pull about six channels out of the "air" here, subscribe to a cable service or buy a satellite dish).

Although there's only one building supply place in town, they don't treat you like they have a corner on the market. Two different times I bought remnant sheet metal roofing (odd sizes) for half the retail price of matching stuff. I remember buying building supplies in my native town of Pasadena, where there's a security guard at the gate to make sure you don't steal anything. In Goldendale, once the yard man knows you he simply trusts you.

When my wife sat on her glasses, the local optometrist interrupted his lunch to fix them. When asked how much it would be, he suggested we make a donation to the local Lions Club!

With all the benefits of small town life, I would be remiss if I failed to mention small towners' love of athletics. Goldendale has, it turns out, a basketball team that everyone supports. The fact that it has a winning record helps, I suppose, but on Friday nights, basketball and football bring out bigger crowds than anything else (outnumbering, I'd vouchsafe, even the patrons of the local bars).

If you still think this isn't enough, well, maybe it isn't. In larger towns like Bend (population 27,000), there are malls, movie theaters and a community college. Goldendale may never have those things. We do get an occasional "fix" (and avoid paying sales taxes!) by going across the border into Oregon to The Dalles, about 30 miles away. Admittedly, a day there every two to three weeks is a nice break from video movies and a downtown you can walk through in five minutes.

Important Tip

If you're going through cultural withdrawal, you can plan occasional trips to the big or little city for a "fix"! You can also get involved in your local community and help *start* a volunteer theater group (see *Backwoods Home* magazine, March/April 1995), serve on a dance committee and so on. Too many of us forget that we can create our own culture.

PROJECTING FIVE OR MORE YEARS DOWN THE ROAD

You can't always know if the place you've targeted to move to will end up being your final stop. I certainly never planned to do as much moving as I have in my 48 years. I can, of course, rationalize that much of this was fodder for developing an innovative relocation business. But moving is always a struggle. I suppose when you're young—in your 20s and 30s—it can be kind of a lark, even a rite of coming of age. I would certainly not condemn anyone who hasn't "settled down" before they are 30 or so; in this complex age one may well need a third to a half of one's lifetime to sort out one's priorities and actualize them. I feel strongly, however, that we should be able, as I have been, to live where we want—as long as we are willing to make certain trade-offs. And with urban areas eating people whole these days, I believe setting your sights on a town where you can live a balanced life is of paramount importance.

I can't tell you what it would be like to live nearly your whole life in one small city or town. The longest I have stayed in one region that wasn't of my own choosing is six years. There does seem to be a five-year hump—and I've heard it referred to by others. Five years is about right for deciding whether you will stay put or not. In this respect I am still a long way away from knowing if eastern Washington State is "it." (And at the moment, the building officials are giving us a lot of trouble.)

But we're digging in for the long haul—buying land, trying to build a house and endeavoring to expand the business in ways we never have before. I hope you are in a position to make a real investment in a community. It should pay dividends that being somewhat "transient" simply can't.

By buying this book you are probably among something of an "elite" who can, as I have, choose where to live. Do recognize that those you may join in a small town don't necessarily have these advantages. "Many have remained in small towns, tolerating their intolerances and creating entertainment to enliven their culturally arid lives simply because it seemed there was no choice but to stay," writes John Perry Barlow in *Utne Reader*.

This comment, incidentally, was made in the context of an article about how more and more people are finding "community" via the Internet—and whether it's even remotely the same as being in a small town (Barlow grew up in Pindale, Wyoming). That is a subject for another book!

(I must point out, however, that the Internet is fast becoming a source of information for prospective back-to-small towners. In particular, I know of two bulletin boards relating to living in or moving to the country. See Resources section for information on how to access them.)

I also recognize that in moving to a small town it's important not to bite off more than you can chew. My wife of five years naturally wants to live in the house of her dreams, as do I. But being an owner-builder has its unique challenges that don't always yield to a set time frame. Fortunately, we have a very comfortable and affordable apartment in the meantime. Part of me wants to rush ahead because of my age and the uncertainties of the national and global economy, but a possibly better part of me says, "slow down and smell the roses—the process is paramount, not the end result." Whether you're religious or not, you have to have faith that small, everyday steps will get you where you want to go. And being a small towner, you'll stand out like a sore thumb with a stressed-out city "'tude."

I've done enough moving to believe that anybody who tries to convince you there's only one perfect or ideal place for you is being overly romantic and, frankly, ill informed. I believe we have the capacity to marry ourselves to many places and create meaningful relationships with people everywhere.

Being the world's moving-est people (except for Middle Eastern Bedouins, I suppose), many Americans can't see the value in putting down roots. My advice to you: Don't give up too soon on a place. Or, saying it differently, "Give place a chance." There are many fine small cities and towns out there that won't replicate the Urban/Suburban Nightmare. The longer you stay, the easier it becomes not to leave! Leaving is a prospect that is quite undesirable unless you have unlimited funds, an extraordinarily adaptable spirit, or, as in the old Western ditty, get run out of Dodge on a rail. (You really will have to do some pretty outrageous things for the latter to occur.)

I certainly wish you the best in your quest for a better place to live. Let me know how you are doing and whether I can help further. You can call me directly or write c/o the publishers.

Resources

CHAPTER 1

"Families Need the Hometown Advantage," James Breig, *U.S. Catholic*, April, 1988.

"Eastward Ho," *The New York Times*, September 23, 1993.

"Cities with Heart," Robert V. Levine, *American Demographics*, October, 1993.

The Responsive Community, 2020 Pennsylvania Avenue NW, Ste. 282, Washington, D.C. 20006, 1-800-245-7460 (communitarian movement).

"Children's Stress Index," *ZPG Reporter*, May, 1993, 1400 16th St. NW, Ste. 320, Washington, D.C. 20036, 202-332-2200.

Carrying Capacity Network (CCN), 1325 G Street NW, Ste. 1003, Washington, D.C. 20005-3104, 800-466-4866.

"Choosing a Small Town as a Practice Location," William L. Seavey, *Resident and Staff Physician*, June, 1986.

"Public Attitudes Toward Rural America and Rural Electric Coops," National Rural Electric Cooperative (NRECKA) and the Roper Organization. Available from PR Division, NRECKA, 1800 Massachusetts Ave. NW, Washington, D.C. 20036, 202-8657-9534

The New Corporate Frontier (The Big Move to Small Town USA), David Heenan, McGraw Hill, New York, NY.

CHAPTER 2

Right Choice, Inc. Available from GPI, 1-800-688-6352.

American Chamber of Commerce Research Association (ACCRA), P.O. Box 6749, Louisville, KY 40206-6749, 502-894-9917.

Where To Retire, 1502 Augusta, Ste. 415, Houston, TX 77057, 713-974-6903.

Places Rated Almanac/Location Report/Life in America's Small Cities (see listings in Chapter 4).

The New Corporate Frontier: The Big Move to Small Town USA, David Heenan, McGraw Hill, New York, NY.

Standard & Poors Directory. Look in the reference section of your local public library.

Walker's Manual of Western Corporations.

"How Re-entry Women Can Minimize Negative Images," William L. Seavey, *National Business Employment Weekly* (published by *The Wall Street Journal*), June 3, 1984, 1-800-JOB HUNT (562-4868).

50 Fabulous Places to Raise Your Family, Lee Rosenberg, CFP, and Saralee H. Rosenberg, Career Press, Hawthorne, NJ. Available from GPI, 1-800-688-6352.

Saving on a Shoestring: How To Cut Expenses, Reduce Debt and Stash More Cash, Barbara O'Neill, CFP, Dearborn Financial, Chicago, IL, 1-800-245-2665.

Tightwad Gazette, RR 1, Box 3570, Leeds, ME 04263.

Living Cheap News, P.O. Box 700058, San Jose, CA 95170.

Simple Living News, P.O. Box 1884, Jonesboro, GA 30237-1884.

The Institute of Certified Financial Planners, 7600 East Eastman Ave., Ste. 301, Denver, CO 80231-4397, 1-800-282-PLAN (referrals to financial planners in your area).

The Country Club, GPI, 1-800-688-6352. Membership program that includes Hinterland Host List, book called *The Country Club, Eden Seeker's Catalog* and subscription to *Rural Property Investor* newsletter.

Places USA, Fast Forward, Inc. Software program on over 300 communities (mostly metros) in MS DOS format. Available from GPI, 1-800-688-6352.

CHAPTER 3

U.S. Small Business Administration, 409 Third Street SW, Washington, D.C. 20416, 1-800-UASK-SBA.

Working from Home: Everything You Need To Know About Living and Working Under the Same Roof, Paul and Sarah Edwards, Jeremy P. Tarcher/Putnam, New York, NY, 1-800-788-6262.

The Home-Based Entrepreneur: The Complete Guide to Working at Home, Linda Pinson and Jerry Jinnett, Dearborn Financial, Chicago, IL, 1-800-245-2665.

Country Bound!: Trade Your Business Suit Blues for Blue Jean Dreams, Marilyn and Tom Ross, Communication Creativity.

Gil Gordon Associates, 10 Donner Ct., Monmouth Junction, NJ 08852, 908-329-2266.

Mid-Career Entrepreneur: How To Start a Business and Be Your Own Boss, Joseph R. Mancuso, Dearborn Financial, Chicago, IL, 1-800-245-2665.

Retiring to Your Own Business: How You Can Launch a Satisfying, Productive and Prosperous Second Career, Gustav Berle, Ph.D., Puma Publishing, Santa Maria, CA, 805-925-3216.

Rolling Ventures Newsletter, P.O. Box 2190, Pahrump, NV 89041.

How To Find and Buy Your Business in the Country, Frank Kirkpatrick, Storey Communications, Pownall, VT.

The Whole Work Catalog, New Careers Center, Inc., P.O. Box 339, Boulder, CO 80306.

Upstart Small Business Series (includes country-oriented business books such as running a bed and breakfast, antique business, desktop publishing service, resume service and bar/tavern), Dearborn Financial, Chicago, IL, 1-800-245-2665.

American Entrepreneurs Association, 2392 Morse Ave., Irvine, CA 92714, 714-755-4211.

International Franchise Association, 1350 New York Ave. NW, Ste. 900, Washington D.C. 20005, 202-628-8000.

The Country Club: Why Switching from the Big City to the Boondocks Could Be Your Smartest Move Ever, Dale Wildman, Silvercat Publications. Available from GPI (as part of its Country Club package, which includes the *Rural Property Investor Newsletter*, a resume critique, Hinterland Host List, etc.), 1-800-688-6352.

What Color Is Your Parachute? Richard Nelson Bolles, Ten Speed Press, Berkeley, CA, 1-800-841-BOOK.

Country Careers: Successful Ways To Live and Work in the Country, Jerry Germer, John Wiley & Sons, New York, NY, 1-800-CALL WILEY.

"Home Businesses in Paradise," David G. Jensen, *Home Office Computing*, February, 1991.

"Tale from Dropout Hell" (no author listed), *Smart Money*, April 15, 1992.

CHAPTER 4

"The Best Places To Live Now," *Money,* September, 1995.

Places Rated Almanac, David Savageau and Richard Boyer, MacMillan, Indianapolis, IN, 1-800-428-5331.

"Children's Stress Index," *ZPG Reporter,* Zero Population Growth, 1400 16th St. NW, Ste. 320, Washington, D.C. 20036, 202-332-2200.

National Optimum Population Commission, 1070 SE Denman Ave., Corvallis, OR 97333-2006.

The Rating Guide to Life in America's Small Cities, F. Scott Thomas, Prometheus Books, Buffalo, NY. Available from GPI, 1-800-688-6352.

The 100 Best Small Towns in America, Norman Crampton, MacMillan, Indianapolis, IN, 1-800-428-5331.

Small Town Search Letter, 33402 Dosinia Drive, Dana Point, CA 92629, 714-496-1259.

Location Report (Statistics & points of contact for over 800 U.S. cities), available from GPI, 1-800-688-6352.

Worldwide Chamber of Commerce Directory, P.O. Box 1029, Loveland, CO 80539, 303-663-3231.

The Vacation Home Exchange and Hospitality Guide, John Kimbrough, Kimco Communications, 4242 West Dayton, Fresno, CA 93722.

Penturbia: Where Real Estate Will Boom After the Crash of Suburbia, Jack Lessinger, Ph.D., available from GPI, 1-800-688-6352.

CHAPTER 5

Caretaker Gazette, HC 76, Box 4022, Garden Valley, ID 83622, 208-462-3993.

Greener Pastures Expo. Cassette tapes available of nine main speakers on "becoming country bound," selling property, design and construction in rural areas, best counties in West, retiring overseas, starting home-based business, finding job in smaller cities, best U.S. places to retire and meshing your life mission with change of location. GPI, 1-800-688-6352.

The For Sale By Owner Kit, Robert Irwin, Dearborn Financial, Chicago, IL, 1-800-245-2665.

Home Buyers: Lambs to the Slaughter?, Sloan Bashinsky, Menasha Ridge Press, Rt. 3, Box 450, Hillsborough, NC 27278 (how real estate agents, sellers and money lenders can "fleece" you if you aren't cautious).

The Home Buyer's Kit, Edith Lank, Dearborn Financial, Chicago, IL, 1-800-245-2665.

State Budget and Tax News, State Policy Research, Inc., Columbus, OH, 1-800-633-4931.

Architectural Digest, Knapp Communications, 5900 Wilshire Blvd., Los Angeles, CA 90036.

The Real Goods News, 555 Leslie St., Ukiah, CA 95482-3471, 1-800-762-7325.

Old House Journal, Dovetale Publishers, Gloucester, MA, 1-800-462-0211. Also publishes *Old House Interiors*.

Be Your Own Contractor! James M. Shepherd, Dearborn Financial, Chicago, IL, 1-800-245-2665.

Building Systems Council, 1-800-368-5242, ext. 162 (manufactured housing trade group).

Manufactured Houses: Finding and Buying Your Dream House for Less, A.M. Watkins, Dearborn Financial, Chicago, IL, 1-800-245-2665.

Bill Kaysing's Microhouses. Call 1-800-888-9098 for credit card orders of plan #MEP049 (sheds and gable roofed versions) or write Mother Earth News, Dept. 149A, P.O. Box 10941, Des Moines, IA 50340.

Finding and Buying Your Place in the Country, Les Scher and Carol Scher, Dearborn Financial, Chicago, IL, 1-800-245-2665.

The Modern Homestead Manual, Skip Thomsen and Cat Freshwater, Oregon Wordworks, P.O. Box D, Manzanita, OR 97130.

Backwoods Home (magazine), 1257 Siskiyou Blvd., #213, Ashland, OR 97520,

(503) 488-2053.

"Many Rural Regions Growing Again; A Reason: Technology," *The Wall Street Journal*, November 21, 1994.

The Rural Property Investor/Electronic Cottage Connector, available from GPI, 1-800-688-6352.

United National Real Estate, 4700-GRP Belleview, Kansas City, MO 64112, 1-800-999-1020, ext. 368.

CHAPTER 6

Countryside (magazine), N2601 Winter Sports Rd., Withee, WI 54498, 715-785-7979.

The Complete Relocation Kit: Everything You Need To Know about Changing Homes, Jobs and Communities, Reginald R. Honychurch and Howard K. Battles, Dearborn Financial, Chicago, IL, 1-800-245-2665.

Moving? Don't Get Taken for an Expensive Ride, Henry P. Constantino, Transportation Publishing Company, Box 2309-B, Mission Viejo, CA 92690.

Moving: A Complete Checklist and Guide for Relocation, Karen G. Adams, Silver Cat Publications, San Diego, CA, 1-619-299-6774.

The Homeowner's Kit: All the Facts and Tools You Need from Moving In to Moving Out, Robert de Heer, Dearborn Financial, Chicago, IL, 1-800-245-2665.

CHAPTER 7

On accessing the Internet for information about living in small towns and rural areas:

American Online. Key in: 1. Departments; 2. Lifestyles and Interests; 3. The Exchange; 4. Interests/Hobbies (right-hand side picture); 5. Hobbies Board; 6. Homesteading.

Internet. (Agrarian America Community Network.) Access Internet; in address portion of your heading opposite "to" type listserv@nmsu.edu. In text portion type subscribe agrarianamer <your name>. Within a day you will receive a message from listserv@nmsu.edu, and within days after that a message welcoming you online. Once on discussion list, send all communications to agrarianamer@nmsu.edu (service is free).

For information about Greener Pastures Institute's services, call 1-800-688-6352 or 702-382-4847 (counseling and specific books listed above) or send for catalog to Greener Pastures, P.O. Box 2190-1383, Pahrump, NV 89041-2190.

*I*ndex